The Sur
to C
in
Student Kitchen

LEAN
MEAN
KITCHEN
MACHINE

The Survival Guide to Cooking in the Student Kitchen

by

Susan Crook

Edited by Carolyn Humphries

foulsham

LONDON • NEW YORK • TORONTO • SYDNEY

For my parents, with love

● ● ● ● ● ● ●

foulsham

The Publishing House
Bennetts Close, Cippenham, Berkshire, SL1 5AP

ISBN 0-572-02455-X

Designed and phototypeset in Great Britain by Picturesque, Marlow, Bucks.
Printed in Great Britain by Cox & Wyman Ltd, Reading, Berks.

Contents

Introduction

Kitchen survival isn't likely to be top of most people's anxiety list when they leave home for the first time. I'd put it well below concerns about making new friends, impressing them with your music collection, carrying condoms and holding your booze. But eventually gnawing hunger will take over. Man (not to mention woman) can't live by lager and crisps alone.

Moving away from home either to college or work may be your first experience of cooking since you last followed the *Blue Peter* recipe for peppermint creams ten years ago. Mum was probably around to help you then, but now it's just you and your housemates, struggling to survive in a hostile kitchen, deep within enemy territory.

For the first time you're responsible for a home and a budget. How you handle them will make a huge difference to your experience of student life. All you need is a manual to help you through the initial assault course. This book has been designed so that you can get the most out of shared living. It will help you stick to a budget, organise the cleaning, feed yourself instantly, impress your mates with sumptuous dinners and stun the world with wild parties.

A few words of warning through. It isn't easy. Don't be afraid to ask your mum or an older sibling who's already been there and done that for advice. And most importantly, don't go mad on spending at the beginning of term when your purse is full. You can always splash out on a binge at the end of term if you are able to save any money. But the other way round and you could be in dire straits.

Notes on Recipes

- All ingredients are given in metric and imperial measures. Use only one set per recipe, do not swop around.

- Wash all fresh produce before using and peel where appropriate.

- All eggs are size 3 unless otherwise stated.

- All spoon measures are level unless otherwise stated.

- When a handful is called for, use as much of the ingredient as you can comfortably hold in your hand without dropping it all over the floor.

- Washing up guide: at each recipe you will see the following symbol with a number beside it. The number is rated from 1-5 according to how much washing up that recipes makes. 1 is a minimal amount and so on.

A CARING, SHARING HOUSEHOLD

*I*t all seems desperately exciting as you pack up your posters, pots and pans, wave goodbye to a tearful mum and head for a home where you and a bunch of like-minded friends can do anything. But all too often those rosy dreams of shared living disappear under a pile of dirty dishes and rows about who finished the milk. So be realistic, plan ahead and don't be afraid to compromise – this is about sharing, after all.

Planning

Once you've decided who you're going to live with and where, start to sort out the details of HOW you're going to live. Do this simple multiple choice test together and don't fight – it's just for fun. (Take a majority decision on ♥, ✳ or ● and then see below for how to put each one into practice.)

How do you want to organise the cooking?

♥ All cook as a group.
✳ Take turns to cook for each other.
● All cook separately.

Your choice

♥ You've picked the cheapest and most fun way of getting fed, but it does involve everyone being prepared to pull their weight and come up with recipes to suit all tastes and an agreed household budget.

✳ You're giving yourselves more freedom to experiment and there won't be other cooks trying to spoil your broth. This system is also fairly flexible as not every member of the household needs to join in.

● You could end up with a rather unfriendly fridge full of individually named milk bottles and initialled eggs. There also tends to be a lot of waste – so it's more expensive. But it does give you total freedom.

How do you want to organise the shopping?

♥ All shop together.
✳ Buy the basics communally and buy food for the evening meal if it's your turn to cook it.
● Buy the basics communally and food separately.

(NOTE: if you seriously think you should each buy your own basics like loo rolls, then you shouldn't be living together.)

Your choice

♥ You're unlikely to be able to go shopping together so you'll have to rely on one or two people getting enough food for the week. You'll need to have a VERY good idea of what you all like.

❋ This is more practical. There will be problems if one person wants to cook steak while someone else is churning out variations on lentil spaghetti, but it will even out in the end. It allows for some people not to get involved in communal food at all.

● It is worth having a common fund for household necessities like loo rolls and bills (see Chapter 3 for hints on budgets and kitties).

Who's going to wash up?

♥ We'll have a rota.
❋ Whoever cooks that night.
● We'll all do our own as we go along.

Your choice

Washing up (or lack of it) causes more tension in shared households than almost any other issue. Nothing is more frustrating than rushing home for a hot cup of tea before *Neighbours* to discover that there isn't a clean mug in the house.To make things a little easier all the recipes in this book have a washing up graphic guide –number one for the do-it-yourself-under-the-cold-tap wash up through to number five for the friendship-busting baked-on grease.

♥ The rota. Photocopy this one, stick it on the wall and stick to it. Work out how many weeks there are in the term and allocate accordingly in strict rotation.

NAME	MON	TUES	WED	THURS	FRI	SAT	SUN

Be reasonable with each other – if you all have a quick meal then go out for a night on the town, you can't expect one person to stay behind being sad and doing the washing up. But it should be done by the time someone starts cooking the next day. Everyone will have to be helpful about swopping too if someone's away for the night, weekend or going out.

✳ This is quite harsh and you may feel that once you've cooked for the night then the last thing you want to do is go back into the kitchen to wash up. In that case follow the rota above.

● If you're cooking separately then you must do your own washing up too. And no trying to sneak your pile under someone else's – it won't win you any friends.

How are you going to get the cleaning done?

♥ We'll have a rota.
✳ We'll draw straws on who gets what clean and swap round each term.
● We'll all feel so guilty about the mess that we'll spontaneously burst into an energetic round of cleaning.

Your choice

♥ Another rota. Well, if you're going to have a go at one you may as well have another one. Decide what needs cleaning (nothing should need cleaning more than once a week and if you're thorough once a fortnight will be enough) and build your rota around that. The main areas are –

13

kitchen, bathroom, vacuuming, tidying and
dusting.
✳ Less complicated to organise than a rota but it
does mean that one person gets stuck with
scrubbing the loo for a term/month – give them a
nicer job next time.
● Dream on!

What are you going to do if one person doesn't pull their weight?

♥ It won't happen.
✳ Ignore them and hope they go away.
● Face the problem head on.

Your choice

The problem with all these plans is that one person
will be the slacker. You will know who it is – their
bedroom carpet has disappeared under a layer of
grimy socks and congealed cereal bowls and it's only
the second week of term. The problem is that they
don't know who they are. They won't notice the ring
of blackened grime round the bath or mould-
encrusted mugs. Drastic action is called for.

♥ Believe me, it will.
✳ It may work, but pointing out to them that they
are becoming very unpopular is better.
● Try these methods:

- ✔ Communal shouting – if you all shout at them then it doesn't turn into a personal argument.
- ✔ Dump all the washing up they should have done under their duvet.
- ✔ Phone their parents.
- ✔ Don't cook for them – even if they're sitting at the table with everyone else.
- ✔ If they are causing real tension, ask them to leave.

(But do remember these are drastic measures – hopefully it won't get this far.)

Basic equipment

If, like the majority of students, you rent furnished accommodation privately then your landlord is legally bound to supply some household necessities. However, what he gives you and what you'd like to have will probably be poles apart. You'll also find that three people in the house have kettles and no one has a toaster. Tick off what you've got from the list below then fill in gaps by:

- ✔ Dropping hints to your parents.
- ✔ Swapping with friends who have all toasters and no kettles etc.
- ✔ Tracking down the nearest knockdown household goods shop.
- ✔ Checking ads in the local papers.
- ✔ Rooting around in second-hand shops.

A well-equipped kitchen needs . . .

Large frying pan ✔

Small frying pan

Large saucepan

Medium saucepan

Small saucepan

Large plates

Side plates

Pudding/cereal bowls

Knives, forks and
  spoons

Mugs

Teaspoons

Large casserole dish

Small heatproof dish

Small heatproof bowl

Large mixing bowl

Measuring jug

Sieve and/or colander

Two wooden spoons

Small balloon or other
  wire whisk

Tablespoons

Small sharp knife

Bread knife

Chopping board

Corkscrew and bottle
  opener ✔

Potato peeler

Grater

Toaster

Kettle

Oven gloves

Teatowels

Hand towel

Scissors

Dusters

Dish clothes

Washing-up brush

Pan scourers

Lemon squeezer

Can opener

Garlic crusher

Draining spoon

Fish slice

Draining rack

Baking sheet

Roasting tin (pan)

Grill pan

Washing-up liquid

STOCKS AND SHARES

The kitchen is equipped with gleaming utensils and the rotas are pinned to the wall, but the cupboard is bare. Whether you're cooking together or on your own, start building up a collection of basics the whole household can share.

The following list should form the basis of your first happy household trip to the supermarket.

Buying everything on this list between you won't cost the earth and some things will last all year. As a guide buy large sizes of items you use lots – tea, coffee, cereals etc. and items that won't perish. But buy small ones of things that will be used only infrequently or in tiny quantities – chilli powder, herbs etc. Try out supermarkets' own brands too, they're usually much cheaper than well-known brands.

Photocopy the list and stick it up in the kitchen. Put an X in the box when something runs out for an instant shopping list.

The basics

Margarine

Jam (fruit conserve)

Caster (superfine) sugar
(it can be used in drinks
and cooking)

Coffee

Tea bags

Frozen peas (if you've got
a freezer or freezer
compartment in your fridge)

Salt

Pepper

Mixed dried herbs

Chilli powder

Curry powder

Garam masala and/or
ground cumin

Tomato ketchup (catsup)

Mayonnaise

Vinegar (preferably cider, red
or white wine or use malt)

Good quality vegetable oil
(like sunflower or corn)

Olive oil (small bottle)

Small bag of plain
  (all-purpose) flour

Peanut butter (instant
  protein!)

Veggie stock cubes

Dried milk

Soy sauce

Worcester sauce

Small tub of grated
  Parmesan cheese

Made mustard
  (English, Dijon)

Foil

Self-cling plastic film

Washing-up liquid

Bathroom/kitchen
  cleaner

Bin liners

Disposable dish clothes

Kitchen towels

Loo rolls

AND DON'T FORGET FRESH BREAD AND MILK!

Beyond the basics

You may find your attempt at communal living works out so well that you're able to expand the house shopping list to include items that you all cook with on a regular basis. The most common ingredients in this book are:

Canned tomatoes
Garlic/onions
Cheese
Bacon
Carrots
Potatoes
Baked beans
Red lentils
Brown rice
Pasta

Finding fresh foods

There's no point wasting your culinary efforts on manky meat or passée potatoes so:

Don't buy

✘   Fish that has dull scales and eyes or smells fishy (odd that).

✘   Dented cans of meat or fish – they may be slightly cheaper but the contents have been traumatised (fruit and veg are okay though).

✘   Meat with a brown tinge.

✘   Fruit and veg with a label saying "ripe" – it means overripe.

Do buy

✔ Cheap pallets of fruit and veg at the market, but check for rotten ones as soon as you get it home.

✔ Crisp-looking veg without dark brown spots.

✔ Bread that's still slightly warm (although beware of squashing it on the way home and don't expect it to last long!).

Chilling out

All food will last longer if it's kept cool until ready to use, but fridge space is limited so don't keep everything in there. Use your kitchen space sensibly and don't keep any foods too close to the cooker. If you've got a larder cupboard with ventilation use it!

In (the fridge)

milk
veg (at the bottom)
open cans (decant into covered containers)
raspberries
eggs (in the door only)
cheese
meat and fish
mayonnaise
pesto sauce
salad

Out (the fridge)

rice
pasta
all other fruit
onions
potatoes
bread (goes stale quicker in the fridge)
seasonings
garlic
tea and coffee
flour and other dry goods

Keep all raw foods (especially meat) well wrapped and low down in the fridge so it can't drip onto cooked food.

Respect is due to the fridge

Look after your fridge and it will look after you. Keep an eye on the temperature – if your food is coming out with ice crystals in it then it's too cold. But if your milk goes off in a day or so then it's probably not cold enough (or you've bought dodgy milk). Keep it clean – wipe up spills as they occur and keep all smelly foods well wrapped. If the fridge starts to smell, clear everything out, switch it off and let it DEFROST (unless it's self-defrosting). Here's how:

✔ Have lots of bowls and towels ready to catch the water.

✔ If the freezer section is really frosty sit a bowl of hot water in it to get the ice moving quicker.

✔ If you have frozen food you want to keep, wrap it in plastic bags, then in blankets, until the freezer is switched on again.

✔ Wash the inside with warm water that has a tablespoon of bicarbonate of soda dissolved in it.

✔ Leave to dry with the door open.

The dating game

Just about everything you buy in the supermarket these days has a date on it. The label may say:

Display until   (this isn't your problem)

Best before)
Sell by   )   (your problem)
Use by   )

Most of these dates are playing very safe and a bag of
salad a day past its date won't kill you, but do be
especially careful with meat, eggs and processed
foods like paté and margarine. If you find you're
having to throw food away because it's past its date,
then you need to review how much food you're
buying each week – don't over-shop.

You are what you eat

This isn't a lecture about eating healthily, but when
you first start thinking about what you're going to be
buying and eating, spare a thought for what you're
actually putting into your body. It stands to reason
that the better the fuel is, the better the engine will
run. There's a lot of complicated info around on what
you should and shouldn't be eating, but unless you're
doing a course in nutrition, don't worry too much
about it.

Just bear in mind that the majority of your diet should
be based on carbohydrate (i.e. stodge like pasta, bread,
potatoes and rice – and brown really is best) and fresh
veg/fruit with a small amount of protein (meat, fish,
eggs, cheese) and very little fat, salt or sugar. Think of
it as a pyramid of pleasure.

nice stuff:–*salty/sugary/fatty foods*	Eat little
expensive stuff:–*meat, fish, eggs, cheese*	Have some daily
healthy stuff:–*veg, fruit, pulses*	Eat lots
filling stuff:–*bread, pasta, rice, potatoes*	Eat lots

SPEND! SPEND! SPEND!

*A*s a student you will have very little money. This is a fact of life, so get used to it before we go any further. What you need to work out is how to make the best of what you have got so the majority of it can be spent on having fun.

If you decide to shop and eat together it will work out cheaper, although it can be more tempting to splash out on luxuries if the cost is shared than if the money is coming directly from your pocket.

Whichever way you choose to organise your household, you'll need to sort out a way of splitting the cost – even if you're only sharing the electricity bill. The first step is to ask:

Where is all my money going?

You'll ask this question a lot. These are the essential areas of expenditure –

Rent   Food
Electricity bill   Phone bill
Gas bill   Travel

Total

Work out how much you're spending a week on each and it should give you an idea of how much you've got to spend on the nicer things in life – not to mention books and equipment.

Most of the recipes in this book work out at well under £1 a head (but don't forget to budget for breakfast and lunches away from home).

Here kitty, kitty

To cover the shared household bills – electricity, gas, phone, TV rental, food and non-food essentials like bin liners – you need to put aside a fixed sum every week.

The best way to do this is with a kitty. Each of you pays your share each week, either to a jar under someone's bed or – if you want to be sophisticated – set up a household bank account. Both methods involve you having to trust another member of your household enough to look after the money/keep the cheque book. If you don't, don't get involved with a kitty system. If the slacker in your house is claiming impecunity, don't let them get away with not paying. Give them a date – maybe the first of the month – to cough up by. If they still aren't paying up, padlock the fridge and remove their lightbulbs. If they aren't paying for food and electricity, they don't want them, right? Right.

The advantages of the kitty are that it helps you budget over the term and if there's any cash left at the end of term you can have a big booze-up. On the downside, it can lead to questions about who's spending money on what and there's usually one person who treats it as a loan system for emergency drinking sessions.

An alternative way to organise the household budget is to buy the bits and pieces you need and keep a tally in a book. Work out the totals once a month, so the people who are more efficient about buying bread, milk etc. aren't out of pocket for too long. Have a whip-round for big bills.

If you decide not to have a kitty, then it's up to you to keep control of your budget so you're able to pay the bills – even if they come in the last week of term.

Keeping the cost down

There are endless ways to cut corners and live cheaply – finding them yourself is part of the fun of living away from home – but here are my top 10 money-spinning greats.

✔   Check out your local market and make it the focus of shopping trips. Fruit, veg, eggs, cheese and all manner of household goods can be bought at a fraction of supermarket prices.

✔   When you do have to go to the supermarket, go at the end of the day when fresh produce nearing its sell-by date is marked down.

✔   Keep an eye on supermarket special offers – particularly own brands. They often do "three for the price of two" deals which are a bargain for essential items.

✔ Don't ever buy supermarket fruit and veg which is ready packed – simply by picking up a bag and filling it yourself you're saving.

✔ Supermarket prepared food like pizza and lasagne is often cheaper if you buy it frozen rather than from the chill cabinet.

✔ Collect money-off vouchers which come through the door or fall out of newspapers. Some supermarkets will accept vouchers even if you aren't buying that product, though this is getting rarer.

✔ Buy thin-cut bread. No one will notice the difference and you get a few more slices for your money. If it goes stale, sprinkle with a drop of water and then toast.

✔ Remember that electricity costs more than gas – so if you need hot water for cooking, heat it in a saucepan rather than in the electric kettle. In fact if you have a gas hob, don't bother at all with an electric kettle, one that sits on the hob will be cheaper to buy and run. And only heat the amount of water you need.

✔ If you're cooking something that needs the oven, a casserole for example, do baked potatoes and veg in the oven too to save fuel.

✔ Buy seasonally. Even though you can buy fresh goods throughout the year, strawberries cost a fortune in January and about one-tenth of the price in July and the same goes for just about every other fresh product.

BUT I CAN'T EVEN BOIL AN EGG!

If the last thing you cooked was that *Blue Peter* recipe for peppermint creams ten years ago, despair not. Basic cooking is a cinch. Just bear in mind that raw food + heat = delicious hot food and you can't go wrong. It's just a question of knowing how to apply which heat to what food.

The main cooking methods are boiling, steaming, baking, roasting, frying and grilling.

Boiling

You need a saucepan big enough to cook the quantity of food (see below for guidelines on quantities) plus enough room to cover the food in water. The basic principle is to bring a saucepan of water to the boil and add the food. Continue boiling until it's cooked.

Pasta: Use the biggest possible saucepan, fill two-thirds full with water and bring to the boil. Add a dash of oil and a pinch of salt. Pour in pasta and stir occasionally with a wooden spoon. Turn the heat down so the water just simmers (i.e. bubbles gently).

29

Pasta usually takes about 8 minutes to cook, wholemeal pasta takes a little longer. Some people suggest throwing a strand of pasta at the wall to see if it's cooked (if it sticks, it's done), but this can get messy. I suggest lifting a piece out with the wooden spoon, running it under the cold tap and eating it. You don't want pasta to be too soggy. It needs bite. Don't cover the pan or it will boil over.

Eggs: Probably one of the most difficult things to boil. Put the eggs into a saucepan of cold water and bring to the boil. Add a burnt match to the water (sounds mad, but it helps to stop the eggshell cracking). Once the water is boiling, let it simmer for exactly 4 minutes for a firm white and soft yolk, 5 minutes for a firm yolk.

Rice: White rice is tricky to cook, brown is much better behaved, as well as being higher in fibre. Boil a kettle of water and meanwhile heat a tablespoon of oil in the bottom of a saucepan. Add the rice to the oil and stir round for a minute. (This helps to stop it sticking.) Add the water and bring to the boil, stir once then turn down the heat. It should take about 15-20 minutes to cook for white, up to 30 minutes for brown. Don't stir rice too much as it goes mushy. Drain and rinse with boiling water then drain again.

Potatoes: A lot of the goodness is just under the skin, so don't peel them unless you plan to mash them. Just scrub them and take out the blemishes and bumpy bits. Chop into smallish pieces and cover with cold water. Bring to the boil and allow 10-15 minutes cooking time. (Put new baby potatoes into boiling water and cook for 8-10 minutes until soft right through when pierced.) For mash, drain thoroughly and add a splash of milk, a knob of margarine, salt and pepper and beat with a potato masher or fork until soft and fluffy.

Steaming

This is the best way to cook vegetables because it keeps in all the goodness and colour. You don't need a high-tech steamer – a metal colander over a saucepan of boiling water which is then covered with the saucepan lid does the job just as well. Many woks come with a steaming "shelf" too. Cooking time is slightly longer than with boiling, but is justified by the results.

Greens: Remove tough stalks and outer leaves. Rinse, slice finely and pack into the colander or steamer. Bring the water underneath to the boil, put a lid over the steamer and leave for 5 minutes.

Broccoli: Rinse and chop into small pieces, using the stalks as well as the florets. Steam as above.

Carrots: Top, tail and scrape or peel. Cut into slices a matchstick thick. Steam for about three minutes.

Green beans: Rinse, top and tail. Cut in two or three pieces if liked or leave whole. Steam as above.

Oven baking

It's a good idea to pre-heat the oven for 15-20 minutes before putting the food in, especially when cooking cakes and biscuits. If you're using the oven, it's worth cooking more than one dish at the same time as it saves fuel. But remember if you fill your oven up the food will all take slightly longer to cook. A warm oven is also useful for keeping food hot while you wait for everyone to come back from the pub.

Potatoes: Choose large oversized ones – and give them a good scrub. Score the longest side with a sharp knife – to stop the potato splitting and to make it easier to cut open when cooked. Put in an oven pre-heated to 190°C / 375°F / gas mark 5 for one hour. Potatoes will cook very happily at virtually any temperature so if you contemplate having the munchies after a hard night out, put them on at a low heat, so they're ready on your return.

**You can speed up
the cooking process by sticking a metal skewer
through the centre of each potato.**

Apples: Core cooking (tart) apples from top to bottom using a sharp knife and place in a shallow baking tin (pan). Fill the hole with dried fruit, nuts or muesli, sprinkle a tablespoon of sugar and a tablespoon of water over each apple and bake for 30 minutes at around 190°C / 375°F / gas mark 5.

Roasting

This is like baking except you do it in fat or oil.

Meat: Cooking a joint is very expensive but it is delicious, so choose a joint of meat that looks fresh and lean. Leave any string on to hold its shape until it's cooked. Wipe with kitchen paper, put into a roasting tin (pan). Rub over with a little oil unless it has a coating of fat. Allow 225-350 g (8-12 oz) per person if the meat's got bones in and 100-175 g (4-6 oz) per person if it hasn't. Pre-heat the oven to gas 5 / 190°C / 375°F. Roast for 25 minutes per 450 g / 1 lb plus an extra 25 minutes if you want it well done. Reduce by 5 minutes per 450 g / 1 lb for pink in the middle.

**For crisp pork crackling,
score rind in strips with a sharp knife.
Rub with oil and sprinkle with salt. Stand meat on a
rack in the tin (pan) so it is raised out of the dripping
as it cooks.**

Poultry: Nothing is easier to roast than a chicken, and it's cheap too. Make sure it's completely thawed if frozen. Rinse the chicken and take out any bits in the body cavity (giblets). Put the chicken into a roasting tin (pan), rub with oil. Pre-heat the oven to 190°C / 375°F / gas mark 5. Roast for 20 minutes per 450 g / 1 lb plus an extra 20 minutes.

Potatoes: Roast tatties are one of life's great pleasures. Peel more potatoes than you think you

33

need, and boil for 5 minutes. Drain, then chuck them back into the saucepan and shake for about 30 seconds to roughen the edges so they will brown and crisp. Heat 2 tablespoons of oil in a large roasting tin (pan). Add the potatoes and roll them around until coated in oil. Put in the top of the oven while cooking meat. Baby new potatoes can be roasted too. Simply rinse them, roll around in an oiled baking tin (pan) and cook as above.

Veg: Root veg like parsnips and carrots can be roasted in exactly the same way as potatoes, but you don't need to shake them to roughen the edges.

Frying

Pour as thin a layer as possible of vegetable oil into your frying pan (skillet) and heat it gently. Whatever you're frying keep an eye on it – there's a thin line between frying and burning.

Fry chicken, vegeburgers, beefburgers, mushrooms, eggs, sliced courgettes (zucchini). Sausages and bacon can be dry-fried without fat because they have plenty of their own! Use your common sense when it comes to timing – fried food is cooked when it looks cooked.

How to fry the perfect egg: Get the oil hot, but not hissing. Crack in the egg (in a cup first if you're not very good at it) and stop it spreading too far by pushing the white back towards the yolk with a fish slice. As the white cooks, spoon the hot oil across the yolk and onto that bit of white round it that never cooks. Use the fish slice to dish it out.

Grilling

An increasingly popular option in these health-conscious times. Works like frying by cooking food one side at a time, but without the cooking oil. Again, watch the grill very carefully. Always have the grill hot before cooking.

Sausages: Turn frequently for 7-15 minutes, depending on size. Don't prick them.

Bacon: Make little cuts along the fatty edge of the bacon (this stops it curling up) and grill for about 3 minutes each side.

Courgettes (zucchini) and aubergines (eggplants): Top and tail, then slice thinly from top to bottom. Brush both sides of each slice with oil (if you don't have a pastry brush use a scrunched-up piece of kitchen towel dipped in oil) and grill for three minutes each side.

Red, green and yellow (bell) peppers: Top and tail, cut in half vertically and remove the white bits inside. Grill, skin side up, until the skin blackens. Pop the pepper pieces into a plastic bag or wrap in foil (this loosens the skin). After 10 minutes peel the skin off and serve with olive oil or French dressing (see Salads in Chapter 6). Delicious.

Flavouring

Any dish can be improved by being well seasoned. This basically means adding salt and pepper. Taste, season, then taste again. Chilli powder, mixed herbs,

Worcestershire sauce, soy sauce, mustard and curry powder are store cupboard basics which can add masses of flavour. Just add a little to start with, then more if you need to.

Quantities

Very few student kitchens are equipped with sophisticated weighing scales, but the majority of recipe books call for 100 g of this or 13 fl oz of that. Ignore all that stuff – in this book virtually all quantities are given as handfuls or easy-to-measure portions. Don't forget that tbsp = tablespoon; tsp = teaspoon.

If your first attempt at cooking results in a handful of rice between six or enough spaghetti to feed the five thousand, stop and think about how much food you'd like to see on your plate.

As a guide, rice and pasta double in size when cooking, so if you normally eat about 4 tbsp when cooked, use 2 tbsp raw and so on.

Rewriting the recipes

Once you master the basics of cooking, don't be afraid to experiment. A recipe is a guideline, not a commandment. There are no hard and fast rules in this book – if you want something spicy add chilli; if you've got lots of potatoes sitting around boil some up and chuck them into the curry/omelette/soup that's on the go.

I've tried to give alternatives in the recipes which follow, but if it says "add chopped bacon" and you haven't got any or don't eat the stuff – try chopped mushrooms or peppers instead. There are as many variations as there are people to cook them.

Getting saucy

The most easily varied recipes of all are the two basic sauces which will keep you happily fed for years. They are white sauce and tomato sauce – each one can be the basis of many different dishes. Both sauces can be poured over cooked pasta, rice, baked potatoes or even toast. They can be diluted with water to make soup.

White sauce

Put 1 tbsp margarine or vegetable oil in a saucepan. Stir in 1 tbsp of flour. Whisk in 300 ml / $^1/_2$ pt / $1^1/_4$ cups of milk. Bring to the boil, whisking all the time. Season with salt and pepper.

Cheese sauce: add a handful of grated cheese after cooking.

Mushroom sauce: fry a handful of sliced mushrooms in the butter/oil before adding the flour and milk.

Leek/onion sauce: fry one thinly sliced leek/onion as above.

Tomato sauce

Peel and chop an onion. Fry in 1 tbsp oil until it's transparent then add a 400 g / 14 oz can of chopped tomatoes. Boil rapidly for 5 minutes. Season with salt, pepper and a pinch of mixed dried herbs.

Chilli sauce: add ¹/₂ tsp chilli powder to the sauce when you season it.

Italian sauce: fry a handful of sliced mushrooms with the onion and go heavy on the herbs.

Tuna sauce: drain a 185 g / 6¹/₂ oz can of tuna and add to the tomato

Bacon sauce: chop two rashers (slices) bacon and fry with the onion.

HELP! EXAM CRISIS AND FEEDING YOURSELF INSTANTLY

You know that feeling: starving hungry, but not a second to spare from last minute revision/all night essay frenzy or, heaven forbid, actually enjoying yourself. It's time to resort to ready-made food – open a few cans or head for the supermarket chill cabinet.

It really is important to eat properly – if you're starving in an exam you won't be able to think straight. If you really can't face food, take some glucose tablets into the exam room with you and eat them regularly. This will keep your blood sugar high, helping to keep your brain ticking over at a reasonable pace.

During my finals I lived on pasties, salad and samosas from the Indian supermarket round the corner – all instant foods. Try not to start buying prepared ready meals – they cost a fortune and aren't very good for you. Ditto takeaways. A friend of mine revised in a curry house every night for a month. Having seen the size of his gut and his overdraft afterwards I wouldn't recommend it. But there's no harm in spoiling yourself once in a while!

Supermarket sweeps

In times of crisis the supermarket will help you – as long as you don't start helping yourself to overpriced selections of Indian and Chinese nibbles, chicken tikka or prepared tomato sauce for pasta (my tomato sauce recipe on page 38 tastes just as good and costs one-third of the price).

The best value comes from vegetables dishes and basic things like cheese and tomato pizza that you can add your own toppings to. So fill your basket with:

Smarty little packs of ready to stir-fry veg

Sachets of rice with bits in – Thai or Indian style are good and don't cost much. Add some frozen veg and soy sauce or mango chutney

Oriental noodle soup – for very little money you get a pack of noodles which takes three minutes to cook, plus a sachet of flavouring. Add a few frozen peas or any cooked leftover vegetables in the fridge

Simple chill-cabinet meals-for-one like lasagne or cauliflower cheese are a good buy

Tins of veg curry, ratatouille or stir-fry. Serve with rice noodles (they take only minutes to cook)

Baked beans with meatballs or sausages – a stodge-out for pennies

Frozen crispy pancakes

Frozen chilli or curry with rice

Frozen pizza – cheaper than the chilled variety

Hummous, taramasalata or tzatziki – Greek dips that can be served with pitta bread, tortilla chips, cucumber sticks and carrots

Store cupboard standbys

If your store cupboard is reasonably well stocked you should be able to rustle up the following recipes in minutes. All produce minimal washing up and serve one (it's every man for himself in an exam crisis).

CHEESE AND EGG TOASTIES
Serves 1

2 slices of bread
Margarine or butter
Small handful of grated
 cheese
1 or 2 eggs
A toasted sandwich maker

1 Pre-heat the sandwich maker.

2 Butter the bread and put one slice buttered side down in the bottom bit.

3 Sprinkle on the cheese. Then break the egg on top.

4 Split the yolk with a knife (this is the tricky bit) so it runs equally into each section.

5 Top with the other slice of bread and cook.

**If you don't have a sandwich maker:
make up a cheese sandwich,
beat the egg and soak the sandwich in it
on both sides until completely covered.
Fry in a little oil until golden on both sides.**

BAKED BEAN DELUXE
Serves 1

2 slices of bread
Butter or margarine
Marmite
Handful of grated cheese
200 g / 7 oz can of baked beans

1 Toast the bread, butter it and spread with Marmite.
2 Top with cheese and grill (broil) until bubbling.
3 Meanwhile heat the beans. Pour the beans over the toast.

●●●●●●●●

TUNA, MAYO, SWEETCORN
Serves 1

$1/2$ x 185 g / $6^1/_2$ oz can tuna
 in brine, drained
Small 200 g / 7 oz can
 sweetcorn (corn), drained
1 tbsp mayonnaise
Pepper

1 Put the tuna and sweetcorn in a bowl.
2 Add mayonnaise and season with pepper (you won't need salt).
3 Eat as it is out of the bowl or with toast.

Add leftover cooked rice, pasta or potatoes for a filling meal.

VEG BALTI
Serves 1

1 tbsp vegetable oil

Any vegetables you have
to hand – a courgette
(zucchini), piece of cabbage,
carrots, broccoli – chopped small

$^1/_2$ jar balti curry sauce

Portion of instant noodles

1 Heat the oil and add the vegetables. Stir around for 2-3 minutes then add sauce.

2 Let it bubble gently while you cook the noodles.

**If you've got cooked,
leftover vegetables to hand,
chop them up,
add to the sauce
and heat through.**

• • • • • • • •

BEAN BAKE
Serves 1

400 g / 14 oz can bean salad
  or chilli beans
Handful of grated cheese
1 packet ready-salted crisps

1 Heat the beans in a saucepan then put into a
shallow, heatproof dish.

2 Mix the cheese and crisps together and sprinkle on
top.

3 Pop under a pre-heated grill (broiler) for about 5
minutes until cheese bubbles and beans are heated
through.

● ● ● ● ● ● ● ●

BOILED EGG AND PEANUT BUTTER SOLDIERS
Serves 1

1 egg
2 slices of bread
Peanut butter

1 Boil the egg as described in Chapter 4.

2 Meanwhile, toast the bread and smother in peanut
butter.

3 Cut toast into thin strips and dip into egg.

● ● ● ● ● ● ● ●

SPAGHETTI SURPRISE
Serves 1

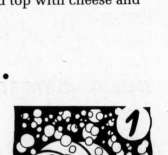

400 g / 14 oz of spaghetti
in tomato sauce

1 surprise item (my mum
uses chopped ham, but a
little tuna, chopped mushrooms or sweetcorn (corn)
would be good)

Small handful of grated cheese

1 slice bread, cut into small cubes

1 Pre-heat the grill (broiler). Heat the spaghetti and
surprise item in a pan.

2 Pour into a heatproof dish and top with cheese and
bread.

3 Grill (broil) for 2 minutes.

• • • • • • • •

TUNA AND MUSHROOM SOUP
Serves 1

1 quantity mushroom sauce
(see page 37)

$^1/_2$ x 185 g / 6$^1/_2$ oz can
tuna in brine, drained

Pepper

To serve: lots of crusty bread

1 Make up the mushroom sauce, but only use 2 tsp
flour. Add the tuna, heat through and season with lots
of pepper. Serve with lots of bread.

MASH AND MUSHROOM SAUCE
Serves 1

1 portion instant mashed
 potato
Lump of butter or margarine
$^1/_2$ x 275 g / 10 oz can
 condensed mushroom soup

1 Make up the potato according to the instructions on
the packet. Add the butter or margarine.

2 Heat soup gently (it will be quite thick) and pour
over.

●●●●●●●●●

HOT MUESLI
Serves 1

Milk
Muesli

1 Fill your favourite cereal bowl with muesli, then
pour the muesli into a saucepan.

2 Fill the cereal bowl with milk, then pour that into
the pan too.

3 Heat gently, stirring all the time, until the muesli
has absorbed most of the milk.

4 Put it back into the cereal bowl. It's like Ready Brek
with bits in.

●●●●●●●●

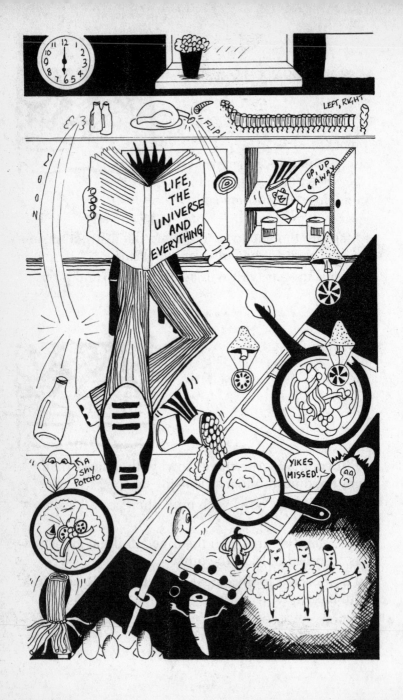

keeping body and soul
together in under 10 minutes

AFTER LECTURES, BEFORE THE PUB

Life's too short to spend too much time in the kitchen. When you need to feed the team quickly, pasta, salads, omelettes and a few ethnic specials do the trick.

Pasta

Pasta really comes into its own when time is short – it's filling, nutritious and CHEAP. All it needs is a sauce and that can be made while it's cooking.

Use a good handful of dry pasta shapes per person – or a 250 g packet for four people. If cooking spaghetti use $^1/_2$ a 500 g packet (or more if you're starving). Cooking time remains the same however much you cook. But make sure you have a large enough saucepan!

Large pasta, like spaghetti or tagliatelle, is best for the clingy sauces – pesto; carbonara; cheese and onion; Moroccan tomato. Short, stumpy pasta shapes are best for chunky sauces – cream, leek and bacon; slacker salmon; chickpea; spinach and mushroom.

49

SLACKER SALMON
Serves 4

250 g / 9 oz pasta shapes
Salt
185 g / 6¹/₂ oz can pink
 salmon, drained and bones and skin removed
2 tbsp cooked peas or sweetcorn (corn) (optional)
4 tbsp mayonnaise
2 tbsp milk
Pepper

1 Cook pasta in plenty of boiling salted water
according to packet directions and drain.

2 Put the salmon in a small pan with the peas or
sweetcorn if using, mayonnaise and the milk.

3 Heat through very, very gently, stirring all the time.
Mix into pasta. Season with pepper.

● ● ● ● ● ● ● ●

CHICKPEA (Garbanzos)
Serves 4

250 g / 9 oz pasta shapes
Salt
2 tbsp olive oil
1 garlic clove, crushed
2 x 430 g / 15¹/₂ oz cans chickpeas, rinsed and drained
1 tsp chilli powder
2 red (bell) peppers, seeded and chopped

1 Cook pasta in plenty of boiling salted water until tender and drain.

2 Heat the oil and mix in all the other ingredients. Heat through for 5 minutes.

3 Add to pasta, toss well and serve.

• • • • • • • •

PESTO
Serves 4

Pesto is one of a growing number of prepared pasta sauces that are a cinch to use and it's probably the best value for money.

250 g / 9 oz large pasta
Salt
2 tbsp pesto sauce
Lump of margarine or
 2 tbsp olive oil
To serve: Grated Parmesan or Cheddar cheese.

1 Cook the pasta in plenty of boiling salted water according to packet directions. Drain and put it back in the pan.

2 Add the pesto and margarine or olive oil.

3 Stir it around and serve with grated Parmesan or Cheddar cheese.

• • • • • • • •

CARBONARA
Serves 4

If you're a garlic fan add a little garlic purée or a
crushed clove with onion.

250 g / 9 oz large pasta
Salt
4 rashers (slices) bacon,
 chopped (or for veggies 2
 handfuls sliced mushroom)
1 tbsp oil
4 eggs
2 tbsp Parmesan, or Cheddar cheese grated
2 tbsp cream or milk

1 Cook pasta in plenty of boiling salted water
according to packet directions. Drain and return to
pan.

2 Meanwhile fry the bacon (or mushrooms) in the oil
until brown.

3 Beat the eggs, cheese, cream or milk and some
pepper in a bowl and stir in the bacon.

4 Add the bacon mix to the hot pasta. Stir it around
over a gentle heat until lightly scrambled but still
creamy and serve with salad.

• • • • • • • •

CHEESE AND ONION
Serves 4

250 g / 9 oz large pasta
Salt
1 onion, chopped
1 tbsp oil
300 ml / ½ pt / 1¼ cups of milk
1 tbsp flour
2 handfuls grated cheese

1 Cook pasta in plenty of boiling salted water according to packet directions and drain.

2 Meanwhile fry (sauté) the onion in the oil until transparent.

3 Add the flour and stir around. Add the milk slowly, stirring as you go. Bring to the boil. Stir all the time until thickened.

4 Add the cheese and stir until melted.

5 Stir into the pasta and serve.

● ● ● ● ● ● ● ●

CREAM, LEEK AND BACON
Serves 4

250 g / 9 oz pasta shapes
Salt
2 large leeks, thinly sliced
4 rashers (slices) bacon, chopped
1 tbsp oil
1 small carton (150 ml / ¼ pt / ⅔ cup) double (heavy)
 cream
Pepper

1 Cook pasta in plenty of boiling salted water
according to packet directions and drain.

2 Fry (sauté) the bacon and leeks in the oil until the
leeks are soft. Add the cream and season with pepper.
Leave to bubble for 2 minutes.

3 Stir into pasta and serve hot.

For a lighter sauce use natural (plain) yoghurt.

• • • • • • • •

MORROCAN TOMATO
Serves 4

250 g / 9 oz pasta shapes
Salt
1 onion, chopped
1 garlic clove, crushed
1 small aubergine (eggplant), topped, tailed and cubed
2 tbsp oil
400 g / 14 oz can chopped tomatoes
1 tbsp raisins or sultanas (golden raisins)
1 tsp ground cumin (optional)

1 Cook pasta in plenty of boiling salted water according to packet directions and drain.

2 Fry (sauté) the onion, garlic and aubergine in the oil for five minutes, stirring.

3 Add the tomatoes, dried fruit and spice and heat through. Simmer for 5 minutes until pulpy.

4 Pile pasta onto warm plates and spoon over, or toss in, the sauce.

●●●●●●●●

SPINACH AND MUSHROOM
Serves 4

250 g / 9 oz pasta shapes
1 tbsp oil
1 garlic clove, crushed
4 handfuls of mushrooms, sliced
4 handfuls of fresh spinach,
 rinsed, de-stalked and chopped
4 large tomatoes, chopped
1 small carton (150 ml / $^{1}/_{4}$ pt / $^{2}/_{3}$ cup) double (heavy)
 cream or thick yoghurt

1 Cook pasta in plenty of boiling salted water
according to packet directions and drain.

2 Lightly fry (sauté) the garlic and mushrooms in the
oil.

3 Add the spinach and tomatoes and keep stirring
until the spinach has wilted. Pour in cream or yoghurt
and heat through but do not boil or it will curdle.

4 Add to pasta, toss and serve.

• • • • • • • •

Salad

Instant, nutritious and almost anything edible can go into it. All good salad needs a good base and a good dressing. Serve with plenty of crusty bread.

The salad base:
This is the veggy bit – any type of lettuce you fancy (washed and torn into pieces), shredded cabbage (red, white or green), sliced cucumber, grated or chopped carrot or other root veggies, sliced tomato, chopped (bell) peppers, sliced mushrooms, lightly boiled cauliflower or broccoli florets, grated courgette (zucchini).
Aim to cover each plate with the stuff then put the tasty bits on top.

The salad dressing:
This is the oily bit – the classic recipe is one part vinegar or lemon juice to three parts olive oil, mixed and shaken well.
This can be altered with splashes of different flavoured oils like walnut and sesame, or soy sauce for an oriental touch.
Always season dressing with salt and pepper.
A crushed garlic clove, a dash of chilli or a pinch of mixed dried herbs is good too.
Salad dressing will keep up to a week in the fridge. 3 tbsp of oil and one of vinegar will serve 4 people.

SPINACH, BACON AND AVOCADO
Serves 4

Salad base for 4 plates
 (see above)
4 small handfuls of spinach
 leaves, washed and torn
 into pieces
4 tbsp olive oil
4 rashers (slices) bacon, chopped, or 4 small handfuls
 of mushrooms, sliced
1 tbsp lemon juice
2 ripe avocados, peeled and chopped

1 Arrange the spinach leaves on the salad base.

2 Heat the oil in a small frying pan (skillet) and fry
(sauté) the bacon or mushrooms until brown.

3 Add the lemon juice then pour the entire contents of
the pan over the spinach (the hot dressing will wilt
the spinach slightly). Chuck the avocado on top and
serve straight away.

**An avocado is ripe
when you can move the skin
around the top with your thumb**

EGGY SALAD
Serves 4

Salad base and dressing
 for 4 plates

4 tomatoes, sliced

4 tbsp mayonnaise

4 eggs

Oil

4 thick slices of bread (white is best), cubed

1 Boil the eggs for around 8 minutes, then place in cold water until cool enough to shell. Quarter the eggs.

2 Put eggs and tomatoes on the salad base and spoon mayonnaise on top.

3 Heat the oil in a small frying pan (skillet). Add the bread. Keep the heat high until the bread is golden and crispy on all sides, stirring all the time.

4 Remove from pan with a draining spoon, drain on kitchen paper then scatter over salad.

**For garlic croutons (bread cubes)
add a crushed clove of garlic
to the oil before frying bread.**

• • • • • • • •

59

MEXICAN PASTA
Serves 4

Salad base for 4 plates
  (see above)

4 handfuls of pasta shapes,
  cooked (see page 49),
  rinsed with cold water and drained

425 g / 15 oz can red kidney beans, washed and
  drained

200 g / 7 oz can sweetcorn (corn), drained

1 ripe avocado, peeled and chopped

Salad dressing (see above) made with one tsp chilli
  powder

1 Mix together the pasta, beans, corn, and avocado.

2 Add the dressing, toss well and spoon onto salad
base.

● ● ● ● ● ● ● ●

HOT CHICKEN AND BACON
Serves 4

Salad base for 4 plates
  (see above)

4 tbsp olive oil

4 rashers (slices) bacon,
  chopped

2 chicken breasts, skinned and cubed

2 tbsp lemon juice

1 Arrange the salad on four plates.

2 Heat the oil in a frying pan (skillet) and fry (sauté) the bacon and chicken, stirring occasionally until both are lightly browned – about 7 minutes. Add the lemon juice and spoon onto salads. Serve straight away.

● ● ● ● ● ● ● ●

HOT 'N' SPICY TOFU
Serves 4

Salad base for 4 plates
2 tbsp soy sauce
1 tsp chilli powder
1 packet of firm silken tofu,
  cubed
2 handfuls of mushrooms, sliced
4 tbsp olive oil
Small, 200 g / 7 oz can sweetcorn (corn), drained and
  rinsed

1 Arrange salad bases on plates.

2 Mix the soy sauce and chilli in a bowl, add the tofu and leave to marinate for 10 minutes.

3 Fry (sauté) the mushrooms in the oil, add the tofu, mix and heat through gently, stirring. Sprinkle the sweetcorn over the salad bases and put the hot tofu mix on top.

● ● ● ● ● ● ● ●

GOAT'S CHEESE AND GRILLED PEPPERS
Serves 4

Salad base for 4 plates
4 red or yellow peppers
Salad dressing enough for
 4 plates of salad base
 (see page 57)
1 round goat's cheese
1 slice of toast, quartered

1 Arrange salad base on plates.

2 Grill the peppers. Peel if preferred. Slice.

3 Put slices on top of the salad and pour the dressing over.

4 Slice the cheese horizontally into four discs and place each one on a quarter of toast slice. Grill (broil) for about 2 minutes or until the cheese browns. Lay on the peppers and serve.

• • • • • • • •

ORIENTAL NOODLE
Serves 4

4 handfuls of rice or egg
  noodles
Salt
4 handfuls of mangetout
  (snow peas)
4 handfuls of bean sprouts
Dressing: 2 tbsp soy sauce
1 level tsp chilli powder
juice of $1/2$ lemon
2 tsp sesame oil
2 tbsp olive oil

1 Cook the rice or noodles in boiling water according
to packet directions. Add mangetout for last 2 minutes'
cooking time. Drain, rinse with cold water and drain
again.

2 Add the bean sprouts and divide between four plates
(or bowls). Put dressing ingredients in a screw-topped
jar and shake well until blended.

3 Pour the dressing over the salad and serve.

• • • • • • • •

Stir fries

You could live on stir-fries all year. They suit meat eaters and veggies, use cheap ingredients, take minutes to cook and never taste the same twice. There are just a few basic rules to remember:

**Prepare all the ingredients
before you start cooking.**

•

**Most vegetables will work in a stir-fry –
(bell) peppers, carrots, bean sprouts,
courgettes (zucchini), cabbage, onions, leeks.
For the meat part try skinned chicken or
turkey breast (or look for prepared stir-fry poultry),
pork (shoulder is cheaper than fillet –
or you could try de-rinding and cutting up belly
rashers into very small pieces) and –
if you're feeling very flush – steak.
Liver and kidneys are ideal too.
Cut all meat in strips (or small pieces for kidneys).
You need very little meat –
2 chicken breasts or 225 g / 8 oz meat will serve four
– the veg is the most important thing.**

•

**All the ingredients need to be cut to the same size.
Aim for chunky batons about 5 cm / 2 in long and
5 mm / ¼ in in width and thickness.
You'll need 6 handfuls for four people –
that's the equivalent of 2 courgettes (zucchini),
4 carrots, 2 (bell) peppers and ½ cabbage.**

The flavour of stir-fry comes from the sauce.
There's loads of room to experiment here –
but the basic ingredients for 4 are:
4 tbsp soy sauce, I tbsp vinegar and I tsp of runny
honey or sugar.
Jazz it up with chilli powder, ground ginger, sherry,
sesame oil or I tbsp prepared sauce like yellow bean
(expensive, but if you use it like this it'll last for ages).
Mix up all the ingredients in a bowl.

•

You must stir-fry on the hob in a wok or
deep-dish frying pan (skillet).
Get it really hot and
then add I tbsp of cooking oil.
Swirl the oil around.

•

If you're using meat,
add to the hot oil and cook for 3 minutes,
then add the veg and cook for a further 2 minutes.
Add the sauce and stir thoroughly for a minute more
before serving.

•

Serve with rice or noodles.

•

That's all there is to it!

• • • • • • • •

Omelettes

Another made-in-minutes meal that suits most people. They're best made individually — but if preferred make one big one using 6-8 eggs and serve a quarter per person. Here's how:

In a bowl beat 2 eggs until they look a bit frothy.
Add 2 tbsp water and season well.

•

Choose a topping if you want one –
grated cheese, chopped ham, sliced mushrooms,
boiled potatoes or simply
a pinch of mixed dried herbs all work well.

•

Heat a small knob of margarine or I tbsp oil
in a non-stick frying pan (skillet).

•

Pour in the egg mix.
Use a wooden spatula to lift and stir the egg
until it sets and browns underneath.
Keep the heat low so it doesn't burn.

•

Add any topping after 2 minutes' cooking.

•

When brown underneath and almost set,
pop it under the grill (broil) to finish off, if liked.

•

Cut into quarters or fold in three and
serve with bread and salad.

• • • • • • • • •

More meals in minutes

CHICKEN IN WINE SAUCE
Serves 4

1 tbsp oil
4 skinned chicken breasts,
  cubed
2 handfuls of mushrooms,
  sliced
1 glass white wine (dregs will do)
Small carton (150 ml / ¹/₄ pt / ²/₃ cup) of double
  (heavy) cream or thick yoghurt

1 Heat the oil in a small frying pan (skillet).

2 Add the chicken and stir it around until it starts to brown (about 2 minutes).

3 Add the wine and mushrooms. Cook over a moderate heat for 5 more minutes. Add the cream, heat through and season well. Serve with rice or pasta. Luxurious, but quick.

**You can use chicken thighs
either whole or cubed,
which are much cheaper.
But remember
they'll take a little longer to cook through.**

• • • • • • • • •

THAI GREENS
Serves 4

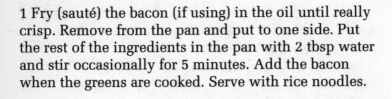

2 rashers (slices) bacon,
  chopped small (optional)
1 tbsp oil
Juice of 1 lime
2 tsp sugar
1 tsp chilli powder
2 tbsp soy sauce
2 heads of greens or one small cabbage, de-stalked and
  shredded
To serve: rice noodles

1 Fry (sauté) the bacon (if using) in the oil until really
crisp. Remove from the pan and put to one side. Put
the rest of the ingredients in the pan with 2 tbsp water
and stir occasionally for 5 minutes. Add the bacon
when the greens are cooked. Serve with rice noodles.

●●●●●●●●

TOMMY EGGS
Serves 4

This recipe was once used
in *Neighbours*. Who says
Aussie soaps have no
cultural worth?

1 onion, finely chopped
4 rashers (slices) bacon, chopped (optional)

1 tbsp oil
6 eggs, beaten
4 tomatoes, seeded and chopped

1 In a saucepan fry (sauté) the onion and bacon (if using) in the oil until the bacon is crisping.
2 Add the eggs and tomatoes and stir around until the eggs are cooked. This is good with chips and ketchup, but toast will do.

●●●●●●●●

MALAYSIAN PEANUT CHICKEN
Serves 4

3 chicken breasts, skinned
 and cut into thin strips
1 tbsp cooking oil
1 green (bell) pepper, cut into thin strips
2 tbsp peanut butter
2 tbsp soy sauce
$1/2$ level tsp chilli powder
To serve: rice or noodles

1 Fry the chicken in the oil until golden.
2 Add the other ingredients and stir until the peanut butter melts.
3 Cook for 5 minutes more, then serve with rice or noodles.

●●●●●●●

SPINACH AND BEAN BHAJI
Serves 4

4 tbsp margarine

2 onions, peeled and
 sliced into fine rings

1 garlic clove, crushed

1 tsp garam masala, ground or cumin

1 tsp ground ginger or chilli powder

2 x 425 g / 15 oz cans red kidney beans, drained and
 rinsed

Lots and lots of spinach – NEVER underestimate how
much spinach cooks down – for this you need at least
900 g / 2 lb.

To serve: natural (plain) yoghurt, naan bread or rice

1 Melt the margarine in a large pan.

2 Fry (sauté) the onion until golden, then add garlic
and spices. Cook for a minute more.

3 Add the beans and spinach. Keep the spinach
moving with a wooden spoon – it'll soon wilt.

4 Serve with natural (plain) yoghurt and naan bread
or rice.

●●●●●●●●

LIGHT MEALS & SNACKS

Not starving, but feel in need of nourishment? Nip into the kitchen and whip up a snack.

VEG STICKS AND AVOCADO DIP

Serves 1-2

Sticks cut from
  peeled carrots,
  cucumber, celery
  and anything else
  you fancy

For the dip:

1 ripe avocado, mashed

1 small carton (150 ml / ¼ pt / ⅔ cup
  natural (plain) yoghurt

½ tsp chilli powder

2 tomatoes and/or a piece of cucumber,
  finely chopped (optional)

1 Mix all the dip ingredients and season
well.

**If you have to leave it around before eating,
put the avocado stone in
to stop it going brown.**

•

71

BLT

Serves 1

This is the classic American sandwich – bacon, lettuce, tomato.

2-3 rashers (slices) bacon
2 slices of bread
Lots of mayonnaise
1 tomato, sliced
Handful of lettuce

1 Grill (broil) the bacon until really crisp.

2 Toast the bread and spread generously with mayonnaise.

3 Pile the tomato and lettuce onto 1 slice of bread, top with bacon then remaining toast.

**Line the grill (broiler) pan with foil
to save those "grilled-on grease"
washing up problems.**

•

**Try substituting the bacon with fish fingers
for an English version.**

• • • • • • • •

BCT

Another variation –
bacon, cheese, tomato.

2 rashers (slices) bacon
2 slices bread
Slices of cheese
1 tomato, sliced

1 Grill (broil) the bacon and put to one side.
2 Toast the bread and top with slices of cheese. Grill the cheese until it bubbles, top with tomatoes, bacon and rest of toast.

• • • • • • • •

PITTA PIZZA
Serves 1

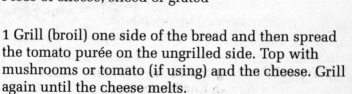

1 large pitta bread
Tomato purée (paste) or
 ketchup (catsup)
Sliced mushrooms or tomato (optional)
Piece of cheese, sliced or grated

1 Grill (broil) one side of the bread and then spread the tomato purée on the ungrilled side. Top with mushrooms or tomato (if using) and the cheese. Grill again until the cheese melts.

• • • • • • • •

MAYO EGGS
Serves 1

Lump of margarine
2 eggs
1 tbsp milk
2 tsp mayonnaise
2 slices of toast

1 Melt the margarine in a saucepan on the lowest possible heat.
2 Add the eggs and beat them with a wooden spoon.
3 Pour in milk and keep stirring all the time.
4 Add mayonnaise and season well. Be patient. Don't turn the heat up or give up the stirring.
5 When the eggs begin to set serve on toast.

● ● ● ● ● ● ● ●

SAUCY MUSHROOMS
Serves 4

Lump of margarine
4 large handfuls of
 mushrooms, sliced
1 tsp mixed dried herbs
2 wine glasses of milk
1 tsp cornstarch, (cornflour) mixed with 1 tbsp water

1 Melt margarine in a saucepan and fry (sauté) mushrooms gently.

2 Add the herbs and milk and cook until the mushrooms start to absorb the milk.

3 Add the blended cornstarch (cornflour) and cook, stirring all the time, until it thickens. Simmer for 1 minute. Serve with toast.

•••••••••

GARLIC BREAD
Serves 4

Totally delicious, but rather anti-social – unless you all eat it!

1 French stick
4 tbsp soft margarine
2 garlic cloves, crushed
1 tsp mixed dried herbs

1 Pre-heat the oven to 190°C / 375°F / gas mark 5.

2 Cut the loaf in half (so it will fit into the oven), then make cuts from the top almost through to the bottom, about 5 cm / 2 in apart. In a bowl, mash the margarine, garlic and herbs together and spread the mixture into the cuts in the loaf. Wrap both halves of the loaf in foil and put in the oven for 15 mins.

•••••••••

Soups

There are two types of soup – creamy ones and clear ones. Creamy ones are made in the same way as the white sauce recipe in Chapter 4, using flour and milk. Clear ones have water and flavouring. You'll need around 900 ml / 1½ pts / 3¾ cups liquid to make soup for four. If in doubt, fill a bowl with milk or water and use that as a measuring guide.

Serve soup with bread and salad for a more substantial meal.

FRENCH ONION SOUP
Serves 4

4 small onions, cut into
very fine rings
2 tbsp margarine
900 ml / 1½ pts/ 3¾ cups water
2 beef stock cubes
2 slices of bread (or 8 thin slices French stick), toasted and quartered
Handful of grated cheese

1 Melt the margarine in a large saucepan and fry (sauté) the onions until soft.

2 Add the water, bring the boil, add stock cubes and simmer gently for 5 minutes.

3 Top the toast quarters with the cheese and grill (broil) until melted. Put two into each bowl and pour the soup on top

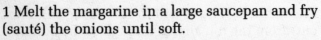

NOODLE SOUP
Serves 4

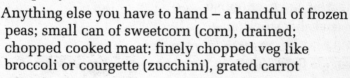

900 ml / 1¹/₂ pts / 3³/₄ cups
 water
2 vegetable stock cubes
4 "blocks" of noodles
1 tsp chilli powder
2 tbsp soy sauce

Anything else you have to hand – a handful of frozen
 peas; small can of sweetcorn (corn), drained;
 chopped cooked meat; finely chopped veg like
 broccoli or courgette (zucchini), grated carrot

1 Boil the water, add stock cubes and stir until
dissolved.

2 Add the noodles and all other ingredients.

3 Boil gently for 3 minutes or follow the instructions
on the packet.

• • • • • • •

BEAN AND BREAD SOUP
Serves 4

1 tbsp oil
2 leeks, thinly sliced
4 large tomatoes, sliced or
 225 g / 8 oz can chopped tomatoes
1 garlic clove, chopped
1 vegetable stock cube
900 ml / 1^1/$_2$ pts / 3^3/$_4$ cups water
425 g / 15 oz butter beans, drained and rinsed
4 slices white bread, cubed
1 tsp vinegar

1 Heat the oil in a saucepan and fry (sauté) leeks over a low heat for 5 minutes.

2 Add the tomatoes and garlic, cook for a further 5 minutes.

3 Add the stock cube and water. Bring to the boil and simmer gently while you add the beans and bread.

4 Switch off the heat and allow soup to stand for 2 minutes before adding vinegar.

Serve straight away.

● ● ● ● ● ● ● ●

MUM, I MISS YOU - A BIT OF HOME COOKING

No one makes it quite like mum, right? Right. Well, now you can have a damned good try. These recipes take longer to cook, so a bit of planning is required, but they are very easy and will delight your housemates – and mum if she comes to visit. All the quantities will serve four, so multiply or divide according to numbers and hunger. All the dishes below should be served with salad or cooked vegetables.

Most of these recipes reheat well, so if you know you'll be in, make double to save time tomorrow. BUT do wait until the cooked food is completely cold before putting it in the fridge. Keep it covered and away from raw food. Reheat in a hot oven until piping hot all through – never just warm until palatable.

If you do burn something DON'T PANIC. A splash of milk can take away the burnt taste of a sauce (be careful not to scrape the blackened base of the pan) and a burnt topping can be scraped off with a pointed knife.

BAKED POTATOES
Serves 4

One of the world's best comfort foods which gives the minimum of washing up. Cook 4 potatoes following the instructions in Chapter 4. Halve, then mash a lump of margarine into each one. Season with salt and pepper then top with:

Cheese: 4 handfuls of grated cheese. Pile on top of potatoes and grill (broil) briefly.

Tuna: Mix a drained 150 g / 5 oz can tuna and 200 g / 7 oz can sweetcorn with lots of mayonnaise. OR mix the tuna into a tub of coleslaw. Pile onto potatoes.

Cathy's chilli bean: Heat 400 g / 14 oz can tomatoes, a 425 g / 15 oz can red kidney beans in chilli sauce and 2 handfuls of sliced mushrooms. Simmer gently for 10 minutes. Spoon onto potatoes and sprinkle a little grated cheese over the top.

A canny idea: Try heating a 425 g / 15 oz (approx) can of ratatouille OR baked beans with sausages OR vegetable curry OR condensed mushroom soup. Spoon over potatoes and serve.

SHEPHERD'S PIE
Serves 4

1 large onion, chopped
750 g / 1¹/₂ lb minced
 (ground) beef
2 carrots, grated
200 g / 7 oz can chopped tomatoes
2 large potatoes, chopped
Lump of margarine
1 tbsp milk
Salt and pepper

1 Dry-fry the onion with the meat in a saucepan, stirring until crumbly.

2 Add the carrots and tomatoes. Simmer for 20 mins.

3 Meanwhile boil the potatoes in plenty of salted water and mash with the margarine, the milk and salt and pepper to taste.

4 Pour meat mixture into a heatproof dish and top with potato. Grill (broil) for 5 minutes or until the topping is turning brown.

●

To chop an onion:
The least painful way is to cut the top off the onion then cut it in half from top to bottom.
Lay each half cut side down on the chopping board. Peel off the brown skin and bin it. Hold onto the root base and make cuts from top to root.
Then cut across horizontally into little squares. Discard the root.

● ● ● ● ● ● ● ●

SAUNDERS PIE

This is a cheat's version
of shepherd's pie

400 g / 14 oz can baked beans
350 g / 12 oz can corned beef
Mashed potato as before

1 Mash the corned beef and add to the beans.

2 Heat through in a saucepan, pour into a heatproof
dish and top with potato.

3 Grill (broil) until the potato starts to brown.

• • • • • • • •

VEGGIE SHEPHERD'S PIE

1 tbsp oil
1 large onion, chopped
1 garlic clove, crushed
400 g / 14 oz can ratatouille
425 g / 15 oz can pulses,
 (cooked, dried beans), drained and rinsed
2 carrots, grated
2 large potatoes, chopped
Lump of margarine
Handful of grated cheese
1-2 tbsp milk

1 Heat the oil in a large saucepan.

2 Fry (sauté) the onion until translucent then add garlic, ratatouille, pulses and carrots. Simmer for 5 minutes.

3 Meanwhile boil the potatoes in salted water until tender then mash them with the margarine, cheese and the milk.

4 Season well then pour the vegetable mixture into a heatproof dish and top with potato.

5 Grill (broil) for 5 minutes so the potato browns slightly.

**Pulses are an important part
of a vegetarian diet instead of meat.
Cooking them from their dried state is cheap
but time-consuming –
they need to be soaked overnight
then boiled rapidly for 10 minutes,
before simmering until tender.
Do not add salt.
(Only red lentils can be cooked without soaking.)
Or buy them ready cooked in cans.
Drain and rinse before using.**

●●●●●●●●

CHEAP FISH PIE
Serves 4

450 g / 1 lb of cheap white
 fish (coley, hoki, whiting)

600 ml / 1 pt / 2$\frac{1}{2}$ cups milk

1 leek sliced, or one red (bell)
 pepper, seeded and chopped (optional)

2 large potatoes, diced

3 tbsp margarine

A splash of milk

Salt and pepper

1 tbsp flour

2.5 cm / 1 in thick slab of cheese, chopped

1 Put the fish in a saucepan. Cover with milk, add the vegetables (if using) and poach on a low heat for 10 minutes until fish flakes easily when pushed with a fork.

2 Meanwhile cook the potatoes in boiling salted water until tender.

3 Drain and mash with 1 tbsp of margarine, a splash of milk, salt and pepper.

4 Heat the remaining 2 tbsp of margarine and stir in flour. Lift cooked fish and vegetables from the milk and place in a heatproof dish. Break up with a fork. Discard the skin and any bones.

5 Pour the milk from the fish into the flour mixture. Stir constantly over a moderate heat until thickened. Add the cheese. Pour sauce onto fish and top with the mashed potato. Pop under the grill (broiler) for 5 minutes or until the potato starts to brown.

CAULI CHEESE
Serves 4

1 cauliflower, cut into florets
4 handfuls of pasta shapes
1 tbsp oil
1 tbsp flour
2 handfuls of grated cheese
600 ml / 1 pt / 2$^1/_2$ cups milk
1 tbsp grated Parmesan cheese (optional)

1 Put cauliflower and pasta in a saucepan of boiling water and boil until cooked – approx 8 minutes.

2 Heat the oil, add flour and stir well.

3 Add milk slowly and a handful of the cheese.

4 Drain the pasta and cauliflower, tip into a heatproof dish.

5 Pour on sauce and top with remaining cheese, plus Parmesan (if using).

6 Grill (broil) until the cheese starts bubbling.

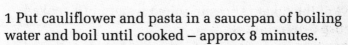

POTATO AND BACON PIE
Serves 4

4 large potatoes, scrubbed
 and sliced
6 rashers (slices) bacon
Oil
4 large tomatoes, sliced
5 cm / 2 in piece Cheddar cheese, thinly sliced

1 Boil the potato slices in salted water until cooked –
about 5-10 minutes.

2 Grill (broil) the bacon until crisp and chop into
small pieces.

3 Oil a heatproof dish and fill with alternate layers of
potato, bacon, tomatoes and cheese. Finish with a
layer of cheese.

4 Bake in the oven at 190°C / 375°F / gas mark 5 for
20 minutes or until hot through, bubbling and golden.

**Once you've opened
a packet of cheese,
wrap the remainder
in foil to stop it going hard.**

● ● ● ● ● ● ● ●

CHEAP CHILLI
Serves 4

1 tbsp oil
1 large onion, chopped
450 g / 1 lb minced (ground) beef
400 g / 14 oz can chopped tomatoes
400 g / 14 oz can red kidney beans, drained and rinsed
1 tsp chilli powder (or less to taste)
4 large handfuls of rice
4 handfuls of chopped lettuce
2 tomatoes, chopped

1 Heat the oil and brown the onion and mince, stirring.

2 Add the tomatoes, beans and chilli powder.

3 Simmer gently for anything between 20 minutes and 2 hours.

4 Cook the rice in boiling, salted water until tender. Drain and divide into bowls or deep plates. Pour on chilli and top with chopped lettuce and tomatoes.

When browning mince, pour off as much fat as you can so it's not too greasy.

• • • • • • • •

SPAGHETTI BOLOGNESE
Serves 4

Garlic clove, crushed
1 onion, chopped
1 tbsp oil
450 g / 1 lb minced
 (ground) beef
400 g / 14 oz can chopped tomatoes
1 tsp mixed dried herbs
4 handfuls of spaghetti (¹/₂ a 500 g packet)
4 tbsp grated Cheddar or Parmesan cheese

1 Brown the garlic and onion in the oil.

2 Add the meat and fry (sauté), stirring until brown and crumbly.

3 Add tomatoes and herbs and simmer for 20 minutes.

4 Cook the spaghetti in plenty of boiling salted water according to packet directions. Drain.

5 Pile on plates, top with meat and sprinkle cheese on top.

• • • • • • • •

SPAGHETTI LENTILESE

Make as for Bolognese, but
 substitute the meat with four
 handfuls of red lentils.

(They don't need browning.)

• • • • • • • •

FRUITY BEAN STEW
Serves 4

1 onion, chopped
1 garlic clove, chopped
1 tbsp oil
1 red and one green (bell)
 pepper, seeded and chopped
2 carrots, peeled and sliced
2 x 425 g / 15 oz cans pulses e.g. black-eyed beans,
 drained and rinsed
400 g / 14 oz can chopped tomatoes
1 orange, peeled and chopped
2 handfuls of raisins or sultanas
4 tbsp orange juice
1 tsp dried mixed herbs
Small (shack-size) bag of sunflower seeds or unsalted
 peanuts (optional)

1 Lightly fry (sauté) the onion and garlic in the oil in a
large saucepan.

2 Add all the other ingredients, except the sunflower
seeds or nuts.

3 Simmer gently for 20 minutes.

4 Top with sunflower seeds or nuts (if using) and
serve with potatoes or rice.

• • • • • • • •

SAUSAGE CASSEROLE
Serves 4

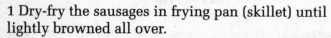

8 large or 12 medium
  sausages (meat or veggie)

1 onion, chopped

4 tomatoes, chopped

2 small apples (Coxes have the best flavour) cored and
  chopped

Apple juice or cider (or half and half)

1 tsp cornflour (cornstarch)

1 Dry-fry the sausages in frying pan (skillet) until
lightly browned all over.

2 Place the onion, tomatoes and apples in a casserole
dish (Dutch oven) and lay the sausages on top.

3 Pour in enough apple juice to half cover the
sausages.

4 Mix the cornflour with 1 tbsp juice or cider and
pour over the casserole. Cover (with foil if you don't
have a lid).

5 Bake for 30 minutes at 190°C / 375°F / gas mark 5.
Remove the cover and cook for 10 minutes more.
Serve with mashed potato.

●●●●●●●●

LIVER AND BACON
Serves 4

2 onions, sliced

1 tbsp oil

4 rashers (slices) bacon

450 g / 1 lb pigs or lamb's liver
1 beef or vegetable stock cube
300 ml / ¹/₂ pt / 1¹/₄ cups water
1 tsp cornflour (cornstarch), mixed into 1 tbsp water.

1 Brown the onion in the oil in a large frying pan.

2 Add the bacon and liver and crumble in the stock cube. Brown gently then pour on the water, and stir in the cornflour mix.

3 Cook over a low heat for 15 minutes. Serve with rice or mashed potato.

•••••••••

CHEESY LAYER
Serves 4

1 tbsp oil
4 carrots, sliced
4 large potatoes, peeled and
 sliced thinly
1 small cabbage, de-stalked and sliced
1 handful of mushrooms, sliced
4 handfuls of green beans – fresh or frozen
2 handfuls of grated cheese
2 eggs
300 ml / ¹/₂ pt / 1¹/₄ cups milk

1 Swirl the oil around in a large heatproof dish.

2 Layer in the veg and cheese, ending with cheese.

3 Beat the eggs into the milk and season well.

4 Pour over the dish and bake for 1 hour at 190°C / 375°F / gas mark 5.

FISH CHOWDER
Serves 4

2 tbsp oil
1 tbsp flour
900 ml / 1½ pts / 3¾ cups
 milk
4 potatoes, diced
225 g / 8 oz smoked fish e.g. haddock or cod
Selection of vegetables – sliced carrots, sliced
 courgettes (zucchini), shredded cabbage, peas,
 chopped tomatoes, watercress, spinach
4 handfuls of grated cheese

1 Heat the oil in a large saucepan.

2 Stir in flour and gradually blend in the milk.

3 Skin the fish: put it skin side down on a chopping
board. Hold firmly one end and work a sharp knife
between the flesh and skin, gradually pushing flesh
back

4 Cut fish into pieces. Put in a pan with the
vegetables.

5 Simmer for about 15 minutes until fish and
vegetables are cooked.

6 Sprinkle cheese over and serve with lots of bread.

●●●●●●●●

SHOWING OFF

Now the kitchen is your oyster (though I wouldn't recommend you go as far as cooking those), let's get a little more sophisticated. However hectic life becomes there will be a time you want to sit down with your mates (or someone you hope to mate with) and have a proper meal.

CHEESE AND AUBERGINE PIE
Serves 4

2 aubergines (eggplants)
Oil
1 onion, chopped
400 g / 14 oz can chopped tomatoes
1 tsp mixed dried herbs
4 handfuls of grated Cheddar cheese
To serve: tagliatelle

1 Top and tail the aubergines then slice into discs slightly thicker than a pound coin (5mm) and prepare as described below (if you have time).

2 Lightly oil a heatproof casserole dish (Dutch oven).

3 Fry (sauté) the onion in 1 tbsp oil until transparent.

4 Add the tomatoes and herbs and cook for five minutes.

5 Spread a thin layer of the tomato sauce on the bottom of the casserole dish. Cover with a layer of aubergine slices. Sprinkle over some of the Cheddar.

6 Continue the layers until you run out of ingredients or the dish is full. Finish with a layer of cheese. Bake in a hot oven at 200°C / 400°F / gas mark 6 for 30 minutes or until vegetables are tender when a knife is pushed down in the centre of the dish. Serve with tagliatelle.

**Aubergines can be bitter
so salting and draining them will improve the taste,
although it's not essential:
slice or cube and place in a colander
over a bowl or the sink.
Sprinkle with salt and leave to stand for 20-30 mins.
Rinse thoroughly then cook as required.**

• • • • • • • •

CHICKEN IN A POT
Serves 4

1.4 kg / 3 lb oven-ready
chicken (completely thawed
if frozen)
1 onion, peeled and quartered
1 lemon, cut into chunks
4 sticks celery, sliced
2 (bell) peppers (red or yellow), seeded and sliced
Small handful of stoned (pitted) olives, rinsed
(optional)
3 garlic cloves, crushed
1/2 bottle dry white wine
1 tsp mixed dried herbs
To serve: potatoes and a green vegetable

1 Remove the giblets from the chicken cavity (if
present) and rinse the chicken and dry with kitchen
paper.
2 Put the onion and half the lemon chunks in the
body cavity.
3 Put the celery, peppers, olives and remaining lemon
in a casserole dish (Dutch oven). Place the chicken on
top, season with salt and pepper and sprinkle over the
garlic and herbs. Pour the wine over the top and cover
with a lid or foil.
4 Cook in the oven at 190°C / 375°F / gas mark 5 for 1
hour 20 minutes. Remove cover and cook for a further
20 minutes. Serve with potatoes and a green vegetable.

• • • • • • • •

THAI VEG CURRY
Serves 4

Salt

2 aubergines (eggplant), cubed

400 ml / 14 fl oz / ¾ cup coconut milk

2 tbsp oil

1 onion, chopped

2 garlic cloves, crushed

2 tbsp Thai red or green curry paste

4 courgettes (zucchini), cut into thick chunks

1 red (bell) pepper, seeded and sliced

Finely grated rind and juice of one lime (or lemon)

1 tsp sugar

2 tbsp soy sauce

To serve: noodles and fresh coriander leaf garnish.

1 Salt and drain the aubergines (if you have time).

2 Open the coconut milk, then leave in the fridge so the cream can rise to the top – don't stir it!

3 Heat oil in a saucepan.

4 Fry (sauté) the onion and garlic lightly, then add the curry paste.

5 Fry until it starts to separate then add prepared veg.

6 Skim off 6 tbsp of thick coconut cream and add to pan. Simmer gently for 10 minutes. Stir in lime rind and juice, sugar and soy.

STUFFED TROUT
Serves 4

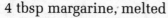

4 tbsp margarine, melted
4 tbsp lemon juice
4 mushrooms, finely chopped
2 slices of bread, crusts removed, finely chopped
4 fresh, cleaned, rainbow trout
Salt and pepper
To serve: potatoes and a green vegetable

1 In a small bowl mix half the margarine, half the lemon juice, the mushrooms and bread. Season with salt and pepper.

2 Rinse the fish and wipe with kitchen paper.

3 Stuff the mushroom mixture into the cavities.

4 Place in a heatproof dish, pour over remaining margarine and lemon and cover with foil or a lid.

4 Cook for 30 minutes at 190°C / 375°F / gas mark 5. Serve with potatoes and a green vegetable.

**For a cheaper dish,
buy mackerel instead of rainbow trout.**

•

**Never re-freeze food.
A lot of fish has been frozen on its way to the shop so
don't store it in the freezer for a later date –
use it as quickly as possible.**

VEGETABLE GOULASH
Serves 4

1 tbsp oil
1 onion, chopped
1 garlic clove, crushed
2 handfuls of broccoli florets
1 red and one green (bell) pepper, seeded and sliced
4 courgettes (zucchini), thickly sliced
$^1/_2$ Savoy cabbage, de-stalked and sliced
2 x 400 g / 14 oz cans tomatoes
2 tbsp sherry
Small carton (150 ml / $^1/_4$ pt / $^2/_3$ cup) soured (dairy sour) cream for garnish
To serve: rice

1 In a large saucepan heat oil and fry (broil) the onion until transparent.

2 Add the garlic, cook briefly then add all the other vegetables. Add sherry and bring to the boil.

3 Turn down the heat and simmer gently for 15 minutes until vegetables are cooked but not soggy. Serve with rice and dollop the cream on top.

**Booze adds lots of flavour to food and
needn't be expensive – any old rubbish will do.
It's worth investing in a bottle of cheap British sherry
just to pep up dishes.
Don't drink it – even in extremis –
the hangover will be horrible!**

STUFFED CHICKEN BREASTS
Serves 4

4 boneless chicken breasts

One red (bell) pepper,
 seeded and thinly sliced

¹/₂ small carton of cream cheese, or 1 garlic and
 herb cheese, like Boursin
 (about 85 g / 3¹/₂ oz)

2 glasses of white wine

To serve: French Potatoes (see page 100) and broccoli

1 Place one chicken breast on a chopping board with
the thickest part facing you. With a sharp knife, make
a small pocket in the side (imagine it's pitta bread and
you're making a donar kebab).

2 Spread a layer of the cheese along the bottom of the
pocket and top with a few strips of pepper. Repeat
with each chicken breast reserving about ¹/₃ of cheese
for the sauce.

3 Carefully place each piece of chicken in a casserole
dish (Dutch oven), closing the "pockets" as you go.

4 Place any remaining pepper strips in the dish as
well. Pour over the wine, cover and bake at 200°C /
400°F / gas mark 6 for 30 minutes until chicken is
cooked through.

5 Put the chicken pieces on plates and stir the
remaining cheese into the wine so it melts to form a
sauce. Spoon over. Serve with French Potatoes and
broccoli.

● ● ● ● ● ● ● ●

FRENCH POTATOES
Serves 4

1 tbsp oil

4 large potatoes,
 sliced thinly

2 large onions,
 sliced into fine rings

Lump of margarine

Salt and pepper

1 mugful milk

1 Swirl the oil into an ovenproof dish.

2 Put a layer of potatoes, a layer of onion rings and a few flakes of margarine into the dish and season with salt and pepper. Repeat until all ingredients are used.

3 Pour over the milk.

4 Bake for 1¼ hours at 200°C / 400°F / gas mark 6.

If serving with stuffed chicken breasts get this dish in the oven before you prepare the chicken.

• • • • • • • •

HOME-MADE PIZZA
Serves 4

2 tsp salt

1 tsp sugar

1 sachet easy-blend
 dried yeast

3 mugfuls flour (preferably
 strong (bread) flour but plain (all-purpose) will do)

100

2 tbsp olive oil

About 450 ml / ¾ pt / 2 cups warm water

Oil for greasing bag

4 tbsp tomato purée (paste)

4 handfuls sliced mushrooms

4 handfuls grated cheese

1 tsp mixed dried herbs

To serve: salad

1 Put the salt, sugar, yeast and flour in a bowl and mix with a wooden spoon.

2 Make a well in the centre, pour in the oil and mix with enough water until the mixture forms a dough which comes away from the sides of the bowl.

3 Place on a floured surface and knead well for a few minutes. Really bash it around (pretend it's someone you hate).

4 Put the dough in a oiled plastic bag. Leave 30 mins.

5 Knead the risen dough for a minute more and divide in two.

6 Flatten each half into a round and place on oiled baking sheets.

7 Spread tomato purée over each one and top with mushrooms, then cheese and herbs.

8 Bake at 230°C / 450°F / gas mark 8 for 15 minutes or until golden and bubbling. Cut up using scissors and serve with salad.

Use an ordinary drinking mug as a measure for flour.

If you don't want to make your own base, buy a ready-made one and brush with olive oil before using (they tend to be a bit dry). Try using grilled sliced peppers and courgettes (zucchini) on top.

VEGGIE PUFF PIE
Serves 4

Flour for dusting
Slab of puff pastry (approx
 250 g / 9 oz), thawed if frozen
1 tbsp oil
2 leeks, sliced thinly
1 red (bell) pepper, seeded and chopped small
4 handfuls sliced mushrooms
2 handfuls of rice, cooked (see page 30) and cooled
2 tbsp soy sauce
1 tsp mixed dried herbs
1 egg, beaten
To serve: salad

1 Sprinkle some flour on a baking sheet or large chopping board.

2 Roll out the pastry until it's about 30 cm/12 in square.

3 Heat oil in a pan and lightly fry (sauté) the leeks, peppers and mushrooms. Add rice, soy sauce and herbs.

4 Rub some oil onto a baking sheet. Place the pastry on it and pile the veg mixture onto one half.

5 Spread a little of the beaten egg around the edge of the pastry (use your finger if you haven't got a pastry brush). Fold over the remaining pastry so it looks like a big Cornish pastie and pinch the edges together well and seal.

6 Brush more egg on the top and make a small slit in

102

the top with a knife (this stops it exploding).

7 Bake for 15-20 minutes at 220°C / 425°F / gas mark 7 until risen and golden brown. Serve with salad.

If you haven't got a rolling pin, use a clean bottle and rub some flour onto it.

●●●●●●●●

CHEESE FONDUE
Serves 4

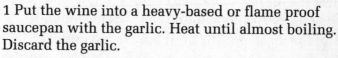

¹/₂ bottle white wine
1 garlic clove, peeled
450 g / 1 lb cheese, grated –
 Cheddar, Emmental or Gruyère
1 tbsp cornflour (cornstarch)
1 French stick, cut into small cubes
Sticks of fresh vegetables like carrots and celery

1 Put the wine into a heavy-based or flame proof saucepan with the garlic. Heat until almost boiling. Discard the garlic.

2 Mix cornflour with cheese and stir into wine. Keep stirring over a gentle heat until it's all melted and the mixture is thick and creamy.

3 Season well and serve in the pan with bread, vegetables and forks for dipping.

First person to drop their bread has to down their drink/buy a round/wash up.

●●●●●●●●

LASAGNE
Serves 4

1 tbsp oil, plus a little for
  greasing
1 onion, chopped
2 garlic cloves, crushed
1 carrot, grated
350 g / 12 oz minced (ground) beef
2 glasses red wine (optional)
150 ml / ¼ pt / ⅔ cup milk
400 g / 14 oz chopped tomatoes
1 tbsp tomato purée (paste)
1 tsp dried mixed herbs
2 packets cheese sauce mix
8-10 sheets no-pre-cook lasagne
2 handfuls of grated cheese
To serve: salad

1 Heat the oil in a large saucepan. Add the onion,
garlic and carrot, cook until they start to colour.

2 Add the meat and stir until brown and crumbly.

3 Pour in wine (if using) and milk and boil rapidly
until most of the liquid has evaporated.

4 Stir in the tomato purée, and herbs. Simmer over a
low heat for 20-30 minutes.

5 Make up cheese sauce mix according to the packet.

6 Oil an oven proof dish, cover the bottom with a thin
layer of meat sauce. Cover with a layer of lasagne. Do
another layer of meat sauce then pasta then some
cheese sauce. Sprinkle on grated cheese and bake for

45 minutes at 190°C / 350°F / gas mark 4 or until lasagne feels soft when a knife is pushed down through the centre. Serve with salad.

• • • • • • • •

PORK CASSEROLE
Serves 4

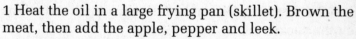

30 ml / 2 tbsp oil
450 g / 1 lb lean, cubed pork
2 apples, cored and chopped
1 red (bell) pepper, seeded and chopped
1 leek, chopped
1 tbsp flour
Apple juice
Salt and pepper
To serve: baked potatoes (see page 32) and spring greens

1 Heat the oil in a large frying pan (skillet). Brown the meat, then add the apple, pepper and leek.

2 Sprinkle over flour and stir well.

3 Turn into a heatproof dish and pour in apple juice until meat is just covered. Season with salt and pepper. Stir well.

4 Cook for at least 1½ hours at 160°C / 325°F / gas mark 3 until tender.

5 Serve with baked potatoes and spring greens.

• • • • • • • •

VEGGIE LASAGNE
Serves 4

30 ml / 2 tbsp oil plus a little
 for greasing
2 garlic cloves, chopped
1 aubergine (eggplant), cubed
2 leeks, sliced
8 handfuls of spinach, rinsed and torn in pieces
4 tomatoes, chopped
1 red (bell) pepper, seeded and chopped
2 small cartons (300 ml / $^1/_2$ pt / $1^1/_4$ cup) natural
 (plain) yoghurt
2 packets cheese sauce mix
8-10 sheets no-pre-cook lasagne
Two handfuls of grated cheese
To serve: salad

1 Heat the oil in a saucepan and lightly fry (sauté) all
the veg for 5 minutes. Mix in the yoghurt.

2 Make up the cheese sauce following the instructions
on the packet.

3 Oil an ovenproof dish and cover the bottom with a
layer of vegetable mix.

4 Then pour over some cheese sauce, cover with
lasagne sheets and repeat the layering process.

5 End with pasta, then cheese sauce and sprinkle over
the grated cheese.

6 Bake for 45 minutes at 180°C / 350°F / gas mark 4
until cooked through. Serve with salad.

● ● ● ● ● ● ● ●

SWEET TREATS

*N*ever trust anyone who says they don't have a sweet tooth. They must be a control freak. Everyone reaches a stage in their life when they need a pudding – don't they?

LEMON ICE CREAM
Serves 4

Large carton (600 ml / 1 pt / 2½ cups) natural (plain) yoghurt
450 g / 1 lb lemon curd
Finely grated rind of 1 lemon (optional)

1 You'll need a large plastic box with a lid (an old plastic ice cream container will do fine).

2 Tip the ingredients into the box and mix really well.

3 Put in the freezer or freezing compartment of the fridge for at least 2 hours (it'll keep for about a month) and take out 15 minutes before you want to eat it.

● ● ● ● ● ● ● ●

FRUIT SALAD BRÛLÉE
Serves 4

Mixed fresh fruit – maybe
  1 banana, 1 apple, 1 orange

425 g / 15 oz can peach
  slices in fruit juice

1 large carton (450 g / 1 lb) fromage frais OR crème
  fraîche OR thick natural (plain) yoghurt

1 small carton (150 ml / ¼ pt / ⅔ cup) of extra thick
  double (heavy) cream

3 tbsp sugar (brown if you've got it)

1 Peel and slice the fruit and put in the bottom of a
heatproof dish. Pour over the peaches and mix well.

2 In a separate bowl, mix the fromage frais/crème
fraîche/yoghurt with the cream.

3 Cover the fruit with the cream mix and sprinkle on
sugar.

4 Get the grill (broiler) really hot and pop the dish
under for a couple of minutes or until the sugar starts
to bubble. Eat immediately or leave to cool then chill
for not much more than 2 hours.

**Puddings are fattening –
you can't get away from it. But you can cut the
calories by substituting
cream with low fat cream substitute,
yoghurt or fromage frais.**

• • • • • • • •

108

FRUIT CRUMBLE
Serves 4

4 handfuls of chopped fresh
 fruit – apples, plums, pears
 and rhubarb all work well

About 3 tbsp sugar (less for
 sweet apples, more for cooking (tart) apples and
 rhubarb)

6 tbsp flour

8 tbsp margarine

4 tbsp sugar

2 tbsp muesli (optional)

To serve: cream or custard

1 Put the fruit into a heatproof dish. Sprinkle over
sugar to taste.

2 Put remaining ingredients in a separate bowl and
rub in with the fingertips (imagine a small blob of
Blu-Tack in your fingers and you'll soon get the hang
of it). Stop when the mixture looks like breadcrumbs.

3 Spoon this on top of the fruit and bake for at least
30-40 minutes at 190°C / 375°F / gas mark 5. Crumble
is very good tempered so it will sit in the oven
happily for longer if need be – just don't let it burn.

4 Serve with cream or custard (the best custard comes
ready made in cartons – don't worry about making it
yourself).

**Experiment with combinations of fruit –
try raisins with apple, soft berry fruits with pear or
orange with rhubarb.**

● ● ● ● ● ● ● ●

MARS BAR SAUCE
Serves 4

3 Mars bars
3 tbsp milk (or cream)
3 tbsp sherry or brandy
Vanilla ice cream

1 Chop the Mars bars small and put in a heatproof bowl with the other ingredients.

2 Put bowl over a saucepan of gently simmering water.

3 Stir gently until the Mars bars have melted. Pour over ice cream and enjoy.

● ● ● ● ● ● ● ●

TRIFLE PUDDING
Serves 4

1/2 an un-iced banana or
  carrot loaf
Juice of 1 orange
Slug of sherry (optional)
3 bananas
3 small cartons (150 ml / 1/4 pt / 2/3 cup) of "custard-style" fruit yoghurt
Small carton (150 ml / 1/4 pt / 2/3 cup) extra thick double (heavy) cream
Kiwi fruit, sliced or a little drinking chocolate powder (optional)

1 Slice loaf thinly and line a bowl with it. Pour over juice (and sherry if using), so the bread is well soaked.

2 Peel and slice bananas, sprinkle over bread.

3 Pour over yoghurt and top with cream. Decorate with peeled and sliced kiwi fruit or a dusting of chocolate powder if liked just before serving.

• • • • • • • •

BREAD AND BUTTER PUDDING
Serves 4

Small lump of margarine
4 slices of bread, buttered
 and quartered
Handful of dried fruit
3 (size 4 or 5) eggs
600 ml / 1 pt / 2¹/₂ cups milk
4 tbsp sugar

1 Rub the margarine around a heatproof dish.

2 Arrange the bread in the bottom of the dish and sprinkle dried fruit over it.

3 Beat eggs, milk and sugar together.

4 Pour over the bread and leave to soak for 30 minutes (if you have time).

5 Bake in the oven at 180°C / 350°F / gas mark 4 for 40 minutes or until the centre has set and top is crisp and golden.

• • • • • • • •

CHOCOLATE FONDUE
Serves 4

Large bar (about 200 g / 7 oz)
 plain (semi-sweet) chocolate

Small carton (150 ml / ¼ pt/
 ⅔ cup) double (heavy) cream

4 tbsp sherry

Fruit for dipping – orange segments, strawberries,
 chunks of banana, sliced pear, grapes

1 Break the chocolate into squares and put in a
heatproof bowl with the cream and sherry.

2 Stand the bowl over a saucepan of gently simmering
water and stir until chocolate melts (don't let it get too
hot or it will go grainy).

3 Give everyone a plate of fruit and a fork to make
dipping easier. If the chocolate starts to solidify, pop it
back onto the saucepan for a minute and stir well.

**Cut fruit goes brown very quickly,
so leave chopping until the last minute or
sprinkle the fruit with lemon juice.
(The lemon juice trick works
for avocados too.)**

BAKED STUFFED PEACHES
Serves 4

4 ripe peaches OR large (600 g
  / 1¼ lb) can of peach halves
  in juice

Small carton (175 g / 6 oz)
  cream cheese

4 tbsp chopped mixed nuts

5 tbsp sugar

1 Carefully peel the peaches, halve and remove stones
(pits) OR drain juice from canned ones.

2 In a small bowl, mix cheese, nuts and 1 tbsp of the
sugar. Stuff the cheese mix into the hole in the peach
where the stone was. Sprinkle remaining sugar over
the peaches. Place the peach halves, stuffed side up,
in a heatproof dish and bake for 10 minutes at 160°C /
325°F / gas mark 3.

**For quickness
flash peaches under a hot grill (broiler)
for 2-3 minutes instead.**

• • • • • • • •

BANANA LOAF

5 tbsp oil plus a little for
 greasing

10 tbsp self-raising wholemeal
(ground) flour

2 handfuls of sultanas
(golden raisins) or raisins

2 heaped tbsp chopped mixed nuts (NOT salted ones!)

3 tbsp sugar

1 tsp baking powder

Pinch of salt

3 ripe bananas

2 eggs, beaten

Juice of 1 orange

To serve: margarine for spreading (optional)

1 Grease a 450 g / 1 lb loaf tin with a little oil.

2 Mix the flour, fruit nuts, sugar, baking powder and salt together in a large bowl.

3 In a separate bowl, mash the bananas with a fork and beat in eggs, oil and 5 tbsp of the juice (it won't look that great at this stage!). Pour this into the dry ingredients and mix well.

4 Spoon into tin and bake for 45 minutes at 180°C / 350°F / gas mark 4. Cover with foil and cook for another 30 minutes or until cooked through.

5 Cool slightly, loosen edge then turn out onto wire rack to cool completely. Serve cut in slices and spread with margarine if liked.

A cake is cooked when a sharp knife in the middle comes out clean.

**If you haven't got a loaf tin,
a small cake tin or heatproof basin
(about 18-20 cm / 7-8 in diameter) will do.**

● ● ● ● ● ● ● ● ●

BANANA BREAD PUDDING
Serves 4

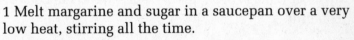

4 tbsp margarine
3 tbsp sugar
Small carton (150 ml / ¼ pt /
²/₃ cup) single (light) cream
4 slices banana bread (see previous recipe)
Vanilla ice cream

1 Melt margarine and sugar in a saucepan over a very low heat, stirring all the time.

2 When it's golden coloured (don't let it go brown) stir in the cream. Keep warm.

3 Toast the banana bread and put each slice on a plate. Top with ice cream and pour over sauce.

This sauce is great poured over slices of orange or coffee ice cream.

● ● ● ● ● ● ● ●

ALL-IN-ONE CHOCCY CAKE

Cake:

Oil for greasing
1 small bar (75 g / 3 oz) plain
 (semi-sweet) chocolate
16 tbsp (1 small 250 g / 9 oz) tub margarine
8 tbsp sugar
3 tbsp milk
8 tbsp self-raising (self-rising) flour
1¹/₂ tbsp baking powder
4 tbsp cocoa (unsweetened chocolate) powder
4 eggs, beaten

Icing:

8 tbsp sugar
1 large bar (200 g / 7 oz) plain (semi-sweet) chocolate
6 tbsp milk

1 Make the cake first: Grease a 20 cm / 8 in cake tin
with oil and then shake some flour around it.
2 Melt the chocolate and margarine very slowly in a
large saucepan. Switch off the heat and mix in the
other ingredients, adding the eggs last.
3 Pour into cake tin and bake for 1 hour at 180°C /
350°F / gas mark 4.
4 Put all the icing ingredients in a saucepan and melt
together. Bring to the boil. Switch off heat and leave to
cool.
5 Once the cake is cooked, remove from oven and

leave to stand for 10 minutes.

6 Carefully turn out onto a wire rack (the grill pan rack will do). When it's cool, cut in half and sandwich back together with a little of the icing. Spread remaining icing over top and sides of cake.

•

**If you're investing in a cake tin
get a deep one with a removable base.**

• • • • • • • •

YUK CAKE

Oil for greasing

8 tbsp margarine

200 g / 7 oz plain chocolate

16 (about 250 g / 9 oz) digestive biscuits (Graham crackers), crushed

1 small bag (100 g / 4 oz) mixed chopped nuts

2 tbsp sugar

1 tbsp sherry or rum (optional)

1 small carton (150 ml / ¹/₄ pt / ²/₃ cup) of double (heavy) cream

1 Lightly oil a 20 cm / 8 in cake tin.

2 Melt margarine in a large saucepan, add chocolate and melt it over a very low heat.

3 Remove from heat, stir in other ingredients and spoon into cake tin. When cold, chill for at least 2 hours or until firm. Turn out and cut in wedges.

• • • • • • • • •

QUICK APPLE CAKE
Serves 4

8 tbsp margarine
7 tbsp sugar
2 eggs, beaten
10 tbsp plain (all-purpose) flour
3 tsp baking powder
2 tbsp orange juice
4 eating apples, peeled, cored and chopped
3 tbsp chopped walnuts

1 Grease a 20 cm / 8 in cake tin with oil and shake some flour around in it.

2 Melt the margarine in a large saucepan, beat in 5 tbsp of the sugar and beat with a wooden spoon or a balloon whisk until the mixture is pale and creamy.

3 Mix in eggs, flour, baking powder and orange juice.

4 Stir the apples into cake mixture.

5 Pour into prepared cake tin. Spread walnuts over top of cake and sprinkle rest of sugar on top.

6 Bake for about 1 hour at 160°C / 325°F / gas mark 3 until centre springs back when lightly pressed and top is golden. Remove from oven and leave to stand. for 10 minutes.

Keep cakes wrapped in foil or in an airtight tin.

• • • • • • •

READY TO PARTY!

Student parties fall into two camps – the ones you're still talking about ten years later and the ones everyone bundles into after the pub and mooches round, optimistically shaking lager cans in the vain hope that they're not all completely empty.

If you want your party to fall into the first category then you need to work out a game plan. Should it be fancy dress or have a theme? What time do you want to have it? Who provides the booze? Getting the alcoholic content of a party right is vital – you want everyone to have a good time without throwing up all over your bathroom.

The best student parties I've been to have been hosted by one household (usually a fairly large one) who've got their act together and provided all the drink and music, then covered the cost by selling tickets to their friends. This means that you know what people are drinking and have control over how many turn up. You do have to be confident that you've bought enough drink and have enough friends to make it economically viable.

Lots of off licences do a drink-or-return deal to help prevent those "out-of-booze" nightmares. But DO keep your drink supplies out of sight – or you could end up with a huge bill and a lot of very drunk people. They will also supply glasses – sometimes free, sometimes for a small hire charge.

If this all seems a bit too organised, then plan a punch and suggest to guests what sort of drink they should bring. You'll need a clean bucket or large washing up bowl, about five bottles of cold white wine, three litres of orange juice and a bottle of cheap brandy. This should keep 10-15 people happy, so multiply according to guest list. Add some chopped fresh fruit to make it look like you've tried and provide soft drinks for drivers and non-drinkers. Don't forget to get enough cups or glasses (paper ones are cheapest).

Do try to keep drinks cold – it makes a big difference. Clear out the fridge and pack it with booze. Even better, see if a tame medical student can get you a great sack of ice (don't ask where from) and fill the bath with it. At worst stand bottles in buckets of cold water outside in the garden if you have one.

•

Stay ahead of the game by drinking lots of water on the night – it really will help prevent a hangover the next day. And don't forget to eat as well as drink.

• • • • • • • •

Some more party themes

◆ Fancy dress can be a laugh: try pop stars; parent of the opposite sex; anything that begins with the letter H (or any other letter of the alphabet); Blackadder characters; soap opera characters; train stations; the Seventies; New Romantics

◆ Try a salsa party: beg, borrow or steal lambada tapes, buy in Mexican beer and set up a tequila bouncer on the door. The bouncer has to give everyone a traditional tequila shot – lick of salt on the back of the hand, shot of tequila and a slice of lemon to bite on. (This can be expensive so it's worth considering charging people for it)

◆ Vodka jelly is another conversation piece: break two packets of lime jelly into cubes and dissolve in 600 ml / 1 pt / 2^1/$_2$ cups vodka. Pour into ice cube trays and chill (it will take a while to set, so start early)

◆ If it's Christmas or New Year, try Gluwein: simmer 600 ml / 1 pt / 2^1/$_2$ cups of orange juice with two cinnamon sticks, a handful of cloves and 4 tbsp sugar for 10 minutes and then strain. In a big saucepan heat one bottle of cheap red wine, 600 ml / 1 pt / 2^1/$_2$ cups water, a large slug of brandy and a ladle of the orange syrup. Alternatively, buy Gluwein sachets (they look like teabags) and follow instructions on the packet

◆ Upside-Downers are guaranteed to make the party go with a swing: you'll need three different spirits – try tequila, vodka and white rum – a bottle of lime cordial and shot measures (egg cups will do).

121

Get the "victim" to lie across a table with their feet facing away from it and the back of their head resting on it. The Upside-Downer Master of Ceremonies pours out one shot of each spirit and one of lime. These are all poured into the victim's mouth. The victim gives them a quick swill then stands up straight WHILE SWALLOWING. Head rush? I should say so. Don't do this late on in a party when guests are already half way out of it. It can be dangerous.

A word of warning

Student parties are notorious for good reason. They're easy to crash and easy to trash. Keep an eye on who knows about your party beforehand and who's coming in on the night. If necessary, get a burly mate to stand on the door and check invitations. You don't want to be the ones losing your deposit on the house or talking to the police at 2 am if things get out of hand.

DO warn your neighbours if it's going to be a biggie because you don't want them calling the police. It's even worth inviting them. They probably won't come but if they've been invited, they're less likely to complain.

Timing of food

If you're not asking guests to turn up until 10 pm or so, it's fair to expect them to have eaten before they arrive. But that means you get the dreaded post-pub crowd, so it can be a good idea to get people to pitch up a bit earlier and then provide them with some food to soak up the alcohol yourself. Of course, this makes the party more expensive, but it also makes it more of

an event and is a good excuse to limit numbers –
perhaps to your corridor in hall or a few of your
favourite neighbouring households.

Party food divides into two sections – easy-to-eat-
with-the-fingers nibbles and huge servings of easily
prepared nosh.

Nibbles

Aim for about 8 nibbles per person

**Make bulk-bought cheap crisps more exciting by
serving them with a dip (see below).**

**Pumpkin and sunflower seeds
can be cheaper than nuts.**

Check out Indian supermarkets for interesting snacks.

• • • • • • • •

MINI PIZZAS

Mini pitta breads
Tomato purée
Mixed dried herbs
Sliced mushrooms
Grated cheese

1 Toast pitta breads on one side, spread purée on the
other. Top with herbs, mushrooms then cheese.
2 Grill (broil) for about 4 minutes or until the cheese
is bubbling. These taste fine cold.

TORTILLA CHIPS, CHEESE AND SALSA
Serves 8

Big bag of tortilla chips
Jar of salsa sauce
4 handfuls grated cheese

1 Put chips onto a heatproof plate or shallow bowl.
2 Spread sauce over the top and sprinkle on cheese.
Grill for about three minutes. Serve quickly.

• • • • • • • •

MINI MEATBALLS
Makes about 20

450 g / 1 lb minced (ground)
 beef
1 egg, beaten
1 garlic clove, peeled and crushed
1 tbsp tomato purée
1 tsp mixed dried herbs
Oil
To serve: dips (see below) and wooden cocktail sticks

1 Mix the first five ingredients together in a bowl. Roll
into little balls.
2 Heat a little oil in a frying pan (skillet) and fry for
about 5 minutes, turning until browned all over. Serve
with a dip.

• • • • • • • •

CURRY SAUCE DIP

1 small carton (150 ml / ¹/₄ pt/
 ²/₃ cup) natural yoghurt
1 small carton (150 ml / ¹/₄ pt/
 ²/₃ cup) double (heavy) cream
2 tbsp mayonnaise
1 or 2 tsp curry powder (depending on your taste)

1 Mix all the ingredients together and serve chilled.

● ● ● ● ● ● ● ●

CUCUMBER DIP

2 small cartons (300 ml / ¹/₂ pt/
 1¹/₄ cup) natural yoghurt
¹/₂ cucumber, grated
1 garlic clove, crushed

1 Mix everything together and serve chilled.

● ● ● ● ● ● ● ●

TOMATO DIP

1 onion, finely chopped
1 tbsp oil
400 g / 14 oz chopped
 tomatoes with garlic and herbs
1 tsp mixed dried herbs

1 Fry (sauté) the onion in the oil until transparent
then add tomatoes and herbs. Boil for 5 minutes then
allow to cool.

Large scale party nosh

**If you don't want to cook,
simply provide loads of French bread,
slabs of cheese and a few pickles.**

•

**Make sure you have enough plates and cutlery for
everyone – borrow like mad or splash out on paper
plates to make the clearing up operation less painful.**

•

**You can feed a lot of people quite cheaply
by bulking out the dishes with lots of stodge – pasta,
potatoes etc. – but if the cost is prohibitive, consider
asking people to contribute a couple of quid.**

TWO SALMON PASTA SALAD
Serves 10

10 handfuls of pasta shapes
– bows look nice
Salt
1 large can (about 400 g / 14 oz) salmon
Small packet of smoked salmon trimmings (from a
 fishmonger – they are much cheaper than a slice)
Small carton (150 ml / $^1/_4$ pt / $^2/_3$ cup) natural (plain)
 yoghurt
5 tbsp mayonnaise
$^1/_2$ small carton (75 g / 5 tbsp) double (heavy) cream
1 garlic clove, crushed
Small bunch of fresh dill (dillweed), chopped
To serve: green salad and lots of bread

1 Cook the pasta in plenty of boiling salted water according to packet directions (use 2 pans if necessary). Drain and rinse with cold water. Drain the can of salmon and chop the smoked salmon, removing any bones and skin from both. Mix all the ingredients together really well. Serve with green salad and fresh bread.

•••••••

CORONATION CHICKEN
Serves 10

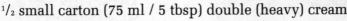

1.75 g / 4 lb oven-ready
 chicken
6 tbsp mayonnaise
1/2 small carton (75 ml / 5 tbsp) double (heavy) cream
3 tbsp mango chutney
2 tsp curry powder
2 handfuls sultanas (golden raisins) or raisins
To serve: green salad and Rice Salad (see page 128)

1 Roast the chicken for 1 hour 40 minutes (see page 33). Leave to cool. (This can be done the day before.)

2 Remove the skin from the chicken and remove as much meat as you can. Chop it up and mix with all the other ingredients.

3 Serve with green salad and rice salad.

•••••••

RICE SALAD
Serves 10

10 handfuls rice
Salt
2 handfuls frozen peas
1 red or green (bell) pepper, finely chopped
1 small can (200 g / 7 oz) sweetcorn (corn), drained
4 tbsp olive oil
2 tbsp vinegar
Salt and pepper

1 Boil the rice in plenty of salted water for 20 minutes or until just tender. Add peas in the last 5 minutes of cooking.

2 Drain and rinse with cold water.

3 Put in a serving bowl and mix in all the other ingredients. Season with salt and pepper.

•••••••••

CLASSY CHILLI
Serves 10

Double the quantities for the Cheap Chilli on page 87. Using two pans if necessary, cook 10 handfuls rice (see page 30 or Rice Salad on this page), drain, rinse with hot water and drain again. Leave rice and chilli in separate saucepans on a low heat on the top of the stove. Let people serve themselves. Put out bowls of garnishes, e.g.

finely chopped lettuce and tomato salad

large carton soured (dairy sour) cream, or natural
 (plain) yoghurt

bowl of grated Cheddar cheese

tortilla chips

Avocado Dip (see page 71)

• • • • • • • •

VEG CHILLI
Serves 10

2 onions, chopped

3 tbsp oil

2 garlic cloves, chopped

2 aubergines (eggplant), cubed

2 courgettes (zucchini), thickly sliced

Large can (350 g / 12 oz) sweetcorn (corn), drained

2 x 425 g / 15 g cans red kidney beans in chilli sauce

400 g / 14 oz can chopped tomatoes

Chilli powder to taste

1 Fry (sauté) the onions in the oil until transparent.

2 Add the garlic, aubergines and courgettes and fry for
2-3 minutes.

3 Add the other ingredients and simmer for 20
minutes. Serve as above, using vegetarian Cheddar.

• • • • • • •

CHICKEN AND CAULI CURRY
Serves 10

2 onions, chopped

3 tbsp oil

2 garlic cloves, chopped

4 tbsp curry powder

20 boneless chicken thighs

1 large carton (300 ml / ¹/₂ pt / 1¹/₄ cups) double (heavy) cream

2 handfuls of red lentils

2 x 400 g / 14 oz cans chopped tomatoes

1 large cauliflower, broken into small florets

To serve: rice (see Chilli on page 30), mango chutney and Cucumber Dip (see page 125)

1 Fry (sauté) the onions in the oil until transparent.

2 Add the garlic, curry powder and chicken, and fry, stirring, for 5 minutes.

3 Add all remaining ingredients except the cauliflower, cover, and cook gently for 20 minutes.

4 Add the cauliflower. Cook, uncovered, for another 10 minutes. Serve with rice, mango chutney, and Cucumber Dip.

•

**Taste your curry near the end of cooking
and, if it's not hot enough,
add chilli powder rather than curry powder –
curry powder needs time to cook properly
to release its flavour.**

• • • • • • • •

VEG CURRY
Serves 10

2 onions, chopped
3 tbsp oil
2 garlic cloves, chopped
6 large potatoes, diced
10 handfuls of spinach, washed and torn into pieces
4 tbsp curry powder
2 x 400 g / 14 oz cans chopped tomatoes
2 tbsp lemon juice
To serve: natural (plain) yoghurt, rice (see Chilli on page 30) and poppadoms

1 Fry (sauté) the onion in the oil until transparent and then add remaining ingredients.
2 Cook, uncovered, for 20 minutes.
3 Serve with yoghurt, rice and poppadoms.

•

**If your curry is too hot,
stir some yoghurt or cream in to cool it down.**

One final party tip

**Don't forget to stock up on loo paper when doing
your party shopping!**
• • • • • • • •

The morning after . . .

So it was a party never to be forgotten, which is strange as you can't remember most of it. The house looks like a bomb site and your head feels like one. Grab a bin liner each, get the Slacker out of bed and give him/her the vacuum cleaner and clear up NOW. Within half an hour the mess will have gone (I promise) and you can contemplate curing your hangover. The best way to do this is with a big FRY UP. It's one of the most difficult things to cook, but follow this minute-by-minute guide and you can't go wrong.

FRY UP –

for four very hungry people

8 sausages/veggie bangers
8 rashers (slices) bacon (or
 hash browns for veggies)
2 x 420 g / 15 oz cans baked beans
Oil
4 handfuls sliced mushrooms
Salt and pepper
Pinch of mixed dried herbs
8 slices of bread
8 eggs
Tea and coffee

FRY-UP MINUS 15 MINUTES. Assemble ingredients, fill kettle, switch grill (broiler) on to medium and oven to 160°C / 325°F / gas mark 3 (if they're separate).

MINUS 14. Place 4 sausages in the centre of the grill (broiler) pan and 4 rashers (slices) of bacon/hash browns round the edge (don't worry if the bacon overlaps – it will shrink). Start cooking.

MINUS 12. Open beans and put in a saucepan ready to go on the cooker. Check on bacon and sausages – turn if necessary.

MINUS 11. Heat about 2 tbsp oil in a large pan (skillet). Fry mushrooms, season with salt and pepper and a pinch of mixed dried herbs, turn into a heatproof bowl and place in bottom of oven to keep warm. Check bacon and sausages, turn sausages again if necessary.

MINUS 10. Put bacon/hash browns and sausages in the oven to keep warm.

MINUS 9. Put on kettle and first round of toast in toaster.

MINUS 8. Put first round of toast in oven along with all the plates you'll be using.

MINUS 6. Put on more toast and rest of bacon/hash browns and sausages. Put 2-3 tbsp oil into frying pan and crack in four eggs. Push the whites together with a fish slice to stop them spreading everywhere.

MINUS 4. Put second round of toast in the oven and start another lot. Check on grill. Get someone else in to make the tea and coffee, get the cutlery and find the ketchup.

MINUS 3. Put first lot of eggs in the oven and start the rest. Ditto toast. Put the heat on under the beans.

MINUS 2. Get warm plates and food out of the oven (use an oven glove) and start dividing up. By the time you've done this, the other eggs, toast and beans will be ready to dish up.

ZERO HOUR. Sit down and get stuck in.

If you really feel so bad after your party-to-end-all-parties that you can't face an onslaught of fat and washing up then drink lots of water, take a painkiller, a vitamin C tablet and try one of these:

FRUIT SHAKE (Serves 1)

Mash a banana in a bowl. Add juice of two oranges and mix well. Pour into a glass and add ice cubes.

PORRIDGE (Serves 1)

Half-fill a mug with porridge oats. Put the oats in a saucepan. Fill the mug with milk or water, pour into pan. Sprinkle in some raisins, if you have some. Heat gently, stirring all the time for 3-4 minutes. Alternatively make Hot Muesli (see page 47).

DRIED FRUIT (Serves 1)

Pour a glass of orange juice into a saucepan. Add a large handful of mixed dried fruit (pear, apple, prunes etc.). Bring to boil and simmer for 15 minutes.

ENTERTAINING

If all this talk of parties sounds a little too raucous for you, then how about entertaining your chums to an elegant dinner party? This involves feeding between six and ten friends with your best recipes and them sitting down, rather than standing up, to get drunk.

Before you even start to think about what to cook consider these questions:

◆   Do I invite my housemates? If not, how are you going to ask them politely to get lost while you entertain more favoured friends? If yes, how many others have you got room for?

◆   Do I have enough cutlery, crockery and chairs for everyone? If you're serving soup and a pudding you'll need a lot of bowls and spoons. Or can you face washing up in the middle?

◆   Am I going to be able to cook everything on my own, or do I need to enlist a willing helper? (Try to get someone else to wash up!)

Menu planning

When you're happy with the logistics, then plan a menu. As you decide on your menu decide on a time plan too. Work out when you intend to start eating and work backwards from there. If your menu is too complicated, find another one. The last thing you want is to be sweating in the kitchen while your guests are having a fine old time without you.

◆   Keep the menu varied – each course should have different flavours and texture. Don't go for dairy product overkill: creamy mushroom soup, followed by pasta with cream, leek and bacon sauce then fruit brûlée.

◆   Don't be afraid to serve old favourites like curry and chilli – just jazz them up a bit with side dishes (see the party section). All sorts of recipes can be upgraded with a bit of thought – extra cream, spices, fresh herbs and slighter better quality ingredients can make all the difference.

◆   Here are some suggested menus to delight your guests with, gathered from recipes in this book. (Increase quantities of ingredients according to numbers.) Each has a rough time guide to help you.

Menu 1 (vegetarian)

AVOCADO DIP WITH CRUNCHY RAW VEG AND TORTILLA CHIPS
(see page 71)
Bump up the chilli powder to make it spicier

SPINACH AND MUSHROOM PASTA (see page 56)

Add a small can of stoned (pitted) olives,
drained and chopped. Serve with salad.

BANANA BREAD PUDDING (see page 115)

TIME PLAN

Earlier that day: cut carrots, cucumbers, peppers etc.
into matchsticks for dip. Make banana bread (or buy
some) and sauce.

1 hour to go: make pasta sauce. Measure pasta into a
saucepan and fill kettle. Prepare all the ingredients for
the dip except avocado and put in serving bowl. Make
salad and dressing, but keep separate.

Just before serving: add avocado to dip ingredients.
Cook pasta, reheat sauce. Assemble salad. Assemble
pudding.

•

**When cooking pasta for a second course like this,
cover it with boiling water or bring to the boil and
then switch the heat off as you serve up the starter –
it should be nearly cooked by the time you start to
assemble the main course.**

• • • • • • • •

Menu 2

GREEK STARTER
Serve shop-bought hummous and taramasalata with Cucumber Dip (see page 125), chunks of cucumber and olives and warm pitta bread cut into fingers.

CHICKEN IN A POT (see page 95)
Serve with baked potatoes (see page 32) and a green veg like broccoli.

CHOCCY CAKE OR YUK CAKE (see page 116 or 117)
Serve with sauce made by sieving a can of raspberries.

TIME PLAN

Earlier that day: prepare the chicken so it's completely ready to go in the oven. Make cake and sauce.

One hour to go: put chicken and potatoes in preheated oven. Prepare green vegetables and put in saucepan.

Just before serving: assemble starter. Steam or boil green vegetables. Assemble pudding.

Menu 3 (vegetarian)

HOT 'N' SPICY TOFU SALAD (see page 61)
Leave out the sweetcorn (corn).

CHEESE AND AUBERGINE PIE (see page 93)
Substitute the Cheddar with a small pack of Mozzarella cheese, chopped, and a small slab of Emmental, grated. Serve with pasta shapes tossed in olive oil or margarine and fresh herbs.

QUICK APPLE CAKE (see page 118)
>Serve with shop-bought apple sauce and crème
fraîche or fromage frais.

TIME PLAN

Earlier that day: make the pie up to the point it goes
into the oven. Make the cake.

One hour to go: marinate the tofu. Assemble salad
ingredients.Put pasta in saucepan and fill kettle.

Just before serving: Cook Tofu Salad. Cook pasta.
Assemble pudding.

Menu 4

FRENCH ONION SOUP (see page 76)
>Substitute stock cubes and water with 2 x 275 g /
10 oz cans consommé (clear beef soup) and 3 tbsp
cooking sherry. Use slices of French stick instead
of ordinary bread (see alternative in recipe).

PASTA WITH CREAM, LEEK AND BACON SAUCE (see page 54)
>Serve with salad.

TRIFLE PUDDING (see page 110)
>Top with slices of kiwi fruit or strawberries.

TIME PLAN

Earlier that day: make pudding and store in fridge.

One hour to go: make pasta sauce. Put pasta in
saucepan so it's ready to go. Make soup up to the
point where you toast the bread. Assemble salad
ingredients.

Just before serving: finish soup. Cook pasta and reheat
sauce. Pour dressing onto salad.

Menu 5 (suitable for vegans)

BEAN AND BREAD SOUP (see page 78)

THAI VEG CURRY (see page 96)
> Try to include fresh coriander, if available.

BAKED STUFFED PEACHES (see page 112)
> Use a soya-based cream cheese.

TIME PLAN

Earlier that day: make soup up to point where you add the bread.

One hour to go: make curry, but don't add coriander. Prepare pudding.

Just before serving: finish soup. Reheat curry and add coriander. Don't put boiling water on noodles until just before serving. Preheat grill, then cook pudding.

Menu 6 (vegetarian)

LEEK AND CHEESE SOUP (see page 77)
> Use blue-veined cheese suitable for vegetarians.

VEGGIE PUFF PIE (see page 102)
> Serve with salad or with green vegetables and boiled potatoes.

FRUIT SALAD BRÛLÉE (see page 108)

TIME PLAN

Earlier that day: make pie and pudding.

One hour to go: make soup. Prepare potatoes and salad/vegetables. Preheat oven.

Just before serving: put potatoes on to boil. Reheat soup and put pie in oven.

Menu 7

SPINACH, BACON AND AVOCADO SALAD (see page 58)
> Don't use too many ingredients in salad base -
> just lettuce (for effect use radicchio) would be OK.

STUFFED TROUT (see page 97)
> Serve with boiled potatoes and broccoli.

BREAD AND BUTTER PUDDING (see page 111)
> Substitute 150 ml / $1/4$ pt / $2/3$ cup milk for double
> (heavy) cream and add 2 tbsp of sherry or brandy.
> Slice a banana, toss in lemon juice and sandwich
> between the bread.

TIME PLAN

Earlier that day: prepare trout. Assemble pudding, but don't cook.

One hour to go: preheat oven. Prepare potatoes and veg. Fry bacon.

Just before serving: assemble salad, put fish and pudding in oven at the same time. Boil potatoes, cook broccoli.

Menu 8

GOAT'S CHEESE AND GRILLED PEPPER SALAD (see page 62)
> Use slices from a French stick as the base for the cheese.

PORK CASSEROLE (see page 105)
> Use cider instead of apple juice. Serve with jacket potatoes and spring greens or mangetout (snow peas).

FRUIT CRUMBLE (see page 109)
> Serve with cream.

TIME PLAN

Earlier that day: grill peppers and leave to marinade in dressing. Assemble casserole and put in fridge. Make crumble topping.

One hour to go: put casserole and potatoes in preheated oven. Assemble pudding.

Just before serving: finish salad and put pudding into oven. Cook vegetables.

Menu 9

NOODLE SOUP (see page 77)
> Use a small bag of defrosted prawns or stick to one vegetable and add some fresh coriander.

STUFFED CHICKEN BREASTS (see page 99)
> Serve with French Potatoes (see page 100) and a green vegetable.

CHOCOLATE FONDUE (see page 112)

TIME PLAN

Earlier that day: prepare chicken breasts and put in fridge. Peel potatoes and leave completely covered in cold water so they don't go brown.

One hour to go: preheat oven. Start cooking potatoes. Make fondue. Defrost prawns.

Just before serving: put chicken in oven. Make soup. Prepare fruit for fondue.

Menu 10 (vegetarian)

TORTILLA CHIPS, CHEESE AND SALSA (see page 124)

VEGETABLE GOULASH (see page 98)
Serve with rice.

MARS BAR SAUCE AND ICE CREAM (see page 110)

TIME PLAN

Earlier that day: make goulash.

One hour to go: grate cheese. Make Mars Bar Sauce.

Just before serving: Cook rice. Assemble starter. Reheat goulash and add cream. Reheat sauce and assemble pudding.

**Stir-fries make good dinner party main courses –
just stick to three main ingredients –
mushrooms, red pepper and meat for example.**

•

**Hot salads can be used as main courses –
serve with lots of good bread.**

Dinner party do's and don'ts

✔   Prepare as much food as you can in advance.

✔   Ask guests to bring booze – but buy some
    yourself in case there isn't enough or it isn't cold.

✔   Chill white wine – chuck it in the freezer for half
    an hour but DON'T forget about it because it will
    explode if you leave it overnight.

✔   Check that your corkscrew works.

✔   Provide mineral water or a jug of iced tap water.

✔   Leave yourself plenty of time to get the food and
    yourself ready – it's bound to take longer than
    you think.

✔   Put candles on the table and play music.

✘   Run out of milk for coffee.

✘   Apologise if things go wrong.

✘   Skimp on quantities.

✘   Cut the bread or dress the salad until the last
    minute.

✘   Panic!

Sunday lunches

Dinner parties don't have to happen in the evenings. Why not invite people round for Sunday lunch like mum makes? They'll love you forever.

Every good Sunday lunch needs:

A roast or casserole
Stuffing
Gravy
A sauce or relish
Roast potatoes
At least two different vegetables
A stodgy pudding

Roast: You'll need a deep roasting tin (pan) to sit the meat in. Follow the cooking instructions on page 33. Add some chopped onion or mixed dried herbs to the pan to add flavour. If you're unsure what sort of meat will roast well, look at guidelines on supermarket packets or ask your butcher, but loin, shoulder or leg are always good bets. When the meat is cooked let it rest for about 10 minutes. This makes it easier to carve and gives you time to make the gravy. If you're cooking vegetarian make deluxe stuffing below.

Chicken is cooked if clear juices run out when you stab the thickest part of the leg with a sharp knife. If they look a bit pink, it needs longer in the oven.

Casseroles: These are a good alternative to a slab of meat. Try the pork casserole (see page 105) or Fruity Bean Stew (see page 89).

Stuffing: Can be made from a packet or with breadcrumbs, melted margarine and flavouring like chopped onion, herbs, lemon juice and chopped apple. Stuffing can be baked separately in a small heatproof dish. If you're cooking for vegetarians as well as meat-eaters, make lots of deluxe stuffing out of wholemeal breadcrumbs, onion, melted butter, a glass of wine, chopped dried apricots and nuts. Serve it as an alternative to the meat.

Gravy: Once the meat is cooked, put it on a large plate and leave to rest. Spoon all but a couple of tbsp of fat out of the roasting tin (leave the juices) and put it on the hob. Sprinkle in 2 tbsp of flour and cook for about four minutes or until it's really brown – keep stirring. Add 450 ml / $^3/_4$ pt / 2 cups of water (preferably from cooking the vegetables) and cook until thick. Make vegetarian gravy by frying a chopped onion in 1 tbsp of oil. Add 1 tbsp of flour then stir in the water, a veggie stock cube and one tbsp of tomato purée (paste).

Sauces: Each type of meat has a traditional accompaniment and they can all be bought virtually ready-made: bread sauce for chicken; apple sauce for pork; mint sauce or redcurrant jelly (clear conserve) for lamb; cranberry sauce for turkey. If you're vegetarian, serve a selection.

Potatoes and vegetables: Follow instruction on page 33 to 34 and don't skimp on quantities – everyone will eat at least five roasties. Oven baked veg will cook alongside the roast – try sliced aubergine (eggplant), courgettes (zucchini) and (bell) peppers with a little crushed garlic and olive oil, cooked in a roasting tin; or shredded red cabbage with raisins, a chopped apple, some sugar and a little water, and a dash of vinegar cooked in a casserole dish (Dutch oven) with a lid.

Pudding: Classic puddings to follow a roast are: bread and butter pudding, fruit crumble and trifle (see pages 109 to 111). Serve with shop-bought custard and cream or ice cream.

TIMINGS

The hardest thing about cooking a roast is getting everything ready at once. Work backwards from the time you want to dish up. Anything that's been cooked in the oven will sit there on a low heat quite happily, so don't panic if you get it a bit wrong. Leave green veg and gravy until the last minute – prepare the ingredients and boil a kettle, then cook them while someone else carves and dishes up the rest of the food.

LEFTOVERS

There are two types of leftovers – the small amount of food left after a meal and the large amount of term left after the money's run out. Both call for drastic measures.

Leftover food

The majority of food that gets left is stodgy – mashed potato, cold rice and pasta.

◆ The easiest thing to do with rice or pasta is to turn it into a salad with some dressing and anything else you have to hand – chopped cucumber, tomatoes, sweetcorn, tuna, canned pulses etc.

◆ Mashed potato can be covered with grated cheese and grilled, or warmed gently in the oven and topped with a fried egg.

◆ Reheat rice or pasta by shoving it into a sieve and steaming over a saucepan of boiling water for 4-5 minutes, stirring occasionally.

◆ Use leftover cooked veg or salad (including dressing) to make a soup with boiling water, a stock cube, soy sauce and noodles.

◆ Spice up boiled eggs or cooked meat with a curry sauce made by frying a chopped onion, a chopped apple and 1 tbsp of curry powder in a little oil. Add 1 tbsp flour and stir. Add 300 ml / ½ pt / 1¼ cups water, a 200 g / 7 oz can chopped tomatoes and 1 tsp lemon juice. Simmer for 10 minutes then add 1 tbsp of natural (plain) yoghurt if you have some.

Leftover term

When the money suddenly seems to run out look to your stock cupboard. You've probably got at least 10 meals staring you in the face right there. But if the cupboard really is bare, call home, see your Student Union Welfare Officer or your bank – no one should go hungry.

If there is SOMETHING in the cupboard try the following – they won't win Michelin stars, but as my mother says, they'll keep the wolf from the door.

POTATO NESTS
Serves 4

4 large potatoes, cut up
Dash of milk
Margarine
Salt and pepper
1 tbsp pesto sauce OR 1 tbsp tomato ketchup (catsup) OR 1 tsp made mustard
4 eggs

1 Boil the potatoes in boiling salted water until tender.

2 When they're cooked, mash them with the milk, margarine, salt and pepper and whichever flavouring you have to hand.

3 Oil a heatproof dish and put the mash in it. Make four little wells in the potato and break an egg into each one. Bake for 10 minutes or until set to your liking.

●●●●●●●●

PANCAKES
Serves 4

4 tbsp flour
1 egg
300 ml / ½ pt / 1¼ cup milk
Oil
Grated cheese OR sugar and lemon juice

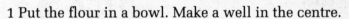

1 Put the flour in a bowl. Make a well in the centre.

2 Add the egg and half the milk.

3 Gradually draw the flour into the liquid, beating as you go until you have a thick batter. Add the rest of the milk. The batter can be left in the fridge for up to 24 hours before cooking.

4 Heat a very little oil in a non-stick frying pan (skillet) and pour off the excess. Add the batter 1 tablespoon at a time, swirling the pan as you go. The secret of making pancakes is to put in as little batter as humanly possibly (usually 2 tbsp). Loosen the sides with a fish slice and toss with a dramatic flourish. Cook underside briefly. Then repeat until all the batter is used. Serve rolled up with cheese or with lemon and sugar.

CARROT AND MARMITE SOUP
Serves 4

2 tbsp oil
3 onions, chopped
4 carrots, grated
4 handfuls of red lentils
Stock cube
900 ml / 1^1/$_2$ pts / 3^3/$_4$ cups water
2 tsp Marmite or other yeast extract

1 Heat the oil in a saucepan and fry (sauté) the onion until transparent. Add the carrot, lentils, stock cube and water. Simmer for 20 minutes. Stir in Marmite and serve.

•••••••••

PEA PASTA
Serves 4

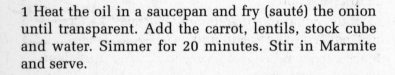

4 handfuls of pasta
Salt
4 handfuls of frozen peas
185 g / 6^1/$_2$ oz can tuna, drained
3 tbsp mayonnaise or double (heavy) cream
Pepper

1 Cook the pasta in plenty of boiling salted water according to packet directions. Add peas for the last 5 minutes of cooking. Drain them quickly then mix in tuna and mayonnaise or cream. Season with pepper.

•••••••••

PEANUT NOODLES
Serves 4

4 blocks quick-cook egg
 noodles
4 tbsp peanut butter
4 tbsp soy sauce
1 tbsp vinegar
1 tsp sugar

1 Cook the noodles in boiling water according to
packet directions.
2 Put the remaining ingredients in a small pan and
heat gently, so the peanut butter melts.
3 Drain the noodles and mix in sauce. Serve straight
away.

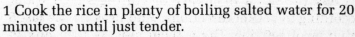

CHEAPO RISOTTO
Serves 4

Six handfuls of rice
Lump of margarine
1 tbsp grated Parmesan
1 tbsp tomato purée (paste) (optional)
Anything else you have around – frozen veg, grated
 carrot, canned pulses, tuna etc.

1 Cook the rice in plenty of boiling salted water for 20
minutes or until just tender.
2 Drain and stir in margarine, cheese and tomato
purée (if using). Add any extra ingredients, heat
through and serve.

VEGGIE CRUMBLE
Serves 4

4 handfuls of any chopped
 veg – carrot, potato, courgette
 (zucchini), aubergine
 (eggplant), cabbage etc.

400 g / 14 oz can chopped tomatoes

1 tsp mixed dried herbs

8 tbsp flour

4 tbsp margarine

Salt and pepper

1 onion, chopped

1 Simmer the vegetables with the tomatoes and herbs for 15 minutes in a covered pan.

2 Put the flour in a bowl with the margarine. Season well with salt and pepper.

3 Rub the fat into the flour with your fingertips as if rolling a small ball of Blu-Tac. When mixture looks like breadcrumbs, stop.

4 Put the tomato mixture into a heatproof dish and top with crumble mix.

5 Bake for 30 minutes at 190ÞC / 375ÞF / gas mark 5 until top is golden brown.

● ● ● ● ● ● ● ●

CHILLI CABBAGE PASTA
Serves 4

4 handfuls of pasta shapes
1 small cabbage, de-stalked
 and shredded
½ tsp chilli powder
 (or more if you like)
2 tbsp grated Parmesan cheese
3 tbsp olive oil

1 Cook pasta in plenty of boiling salted water
according to packet instructions. Add cabbage for last
4 minutes. Drain.

2 Add remaining ingredients and stir.

●●●●●●●●

LENTIL SOUP WITH RICE
Serves 4

4 handfuls of rice
400 g / 14 oz can lentil soup
2 tbsp curry powder
3 onions, sliced into rings
2 tbsp oil

1 Cook the rice in plenty of boiling salted water for 20
minutes or until just tender. Drain.

2 Fry (sauté) onions in the oil slowly until golden.
Heat the soup with the curry powder. Serve rice with
soup poured over. Top with the fried onions.

●●●●●●●●

STALE BREAD SALAD
Serves 4

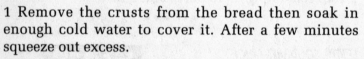

8 slices stale (but not mouldy)
 bread
$1/_2$ cucumber or 1 courgette
 (zucchini), chopped
4 tomatoes, chopped
1 (bell) pepper, seeded and chopped
1 tsp mixed dried herbs
4 tbsp olive oil
2 tbsp vinegar
Salt and pepper

1 Remove the crusts from the bread then soak in enough cold water to cover it. After a few minutes squeeze out excess.

2 Put bread in a bowl and mash with a fork.

3 Add remaining ingredients and mix well.

• • • • • • • •

ONION PIZZA

If you made the pizza recipe in this book when you had more money then you'll probably have the necessary flour and yeast left in the cupboard. Make up a pizza base and cover it with fried onions. French people live on it!

INDEX